T0024054

Reclaiming Cities

Reclaiming Cities

Revolutionary Dimensions
of Political Participation

Yavor Tarinski

Montréal · New York · London

Copyright ©2023 Black Rose Books

Thank you for purchasing this Black Rose Books publication. No part of this book may be reproduced or transmitted in any form, by any means electronic or mechanical including photocopying and recording, or by any information storage or retrieval system–without written permission from the publisher, or, in the case of photocopying or other reprographic copying, a license from the Canadian Copyright Licensing Agency, Access Copyrigh t, with the exception of brief passages quoted by a reviewer in a newspaper or magazine. If you acquired an illicit electronic copy of this book, please consider making a donation to Black Rose Books.

Black Rose Books No. WW431

Library and Archives Canada Cataloguing in Publication

Title: Reclaiming cities : revolutionary dimensions of political participation / Yavor Tarinski.
Names: Tarinski, IAvor, author.
Description: Includes bibliographical references.
Identifiers: Canadiana (print) 20220470316 | Canadiana (ebook) 20220470367 | ISBN 9781551647968
  (hardcover) | ISBN 9781551647944 (softcover) | ISBN 9781551647982 (PDF)
Subjects: LCSH: Metropolitan government. | LCSH: Cities and towns—Political aspects. | LCSH:
  Citizenship—Political aspects. | LCSH: Direct democracy.
Classification: LCC JS50 .T37 2023 | DDC 320.8/5—dc23

Cover design by Associés Libres Design.

C.P. 35788 Succ. Léo Pariseau
Montréal, QC H2X 0A4
CANADA
www.blackrosebooks.com

ORDERING INFORMATION

CANADA / USA	UK / INTERNATIONAL
University of Toronto Press	Central Books
5201 Dufferin Street	50 Freshwater Road
Toronto, ON	Chadwell Heath, London
M3H 5T8	RM8 1RX
1-800-56 5-9523	+44 20 85 25 8800
utpbooks@utpress.utoronto.ca	contactus@centralbooks.com

TABLE OF CONTENTS

Foreword: Cities of hubris

By Chris Spannos

In the play Antigone (442 BCE) Creon, king of the city Thebes, condemns Polyneices's corpse to rot on the battlefield as lawful punishment for the treasonous act of killing his younger brother, Eteocles, who took the throne before Polyneices could. Going against Creon's orders, Polyneices's sister Antigone sought a burial for Polyneices that was consistent with the gods' wishes. In doing so, she placed divine law over human law. The paradox is that by insisting on the punishment of letting Polyneices's corpse rot Creon, who upholds the city's laws, demonstrates his willingness to be alone in thinking that he is right. As such, he transgresses collective wisdom and becomes a man without a city. But Antigone is also without a city as she flouts the city's laws to champion divine laws. In these ways, both Creon and Antigone commit hubris.

For Castoriadis, this play illustrates how justice of the gods does not suffice any more than do the laws of the land suffice. In obeying these laws, people must know that they do not define exclusively what is permitted and that they do not exhaust, either, what is forbidden (Castoriadis 2007: 13–19). The play exhibits the uncertainty pervading political action and democratic frameworks as it "sketches the impurity of motives" and "exposes the inconclusive character of the reasoning upon which we base our decisions" (Castoriadis 1997: 286). Rather than being just a cultural phenomenon, the ancient role of tragedy served to illuminate that human intentions, as causes, are unable to guarantee the production of positive and corresponding outcomes. This is especially pertinent for individuals who are alone in thinking they are right. For, tragedy shows "not only that we are not masters of the consequences of our actions but that we are not even masters of their meaning" (Castoriadis 1997: 284). Thus, aside from exposing the dangers of hubris, tragedy also exposed the need for collective wisdom (Klimis 2014).

Collective wisdom is necessary to fulfill common objectives and public endeavors in a city. Thus, it is a citizen's role to help arrive at this collective wisdom. However uncertain the outcomes of the autonomous project may be, it is the process of public creation and deliberation which is how a directly democratic society reabsorbs the political as explicit power back into politics "as the lucid and deliberate activity whose object is the explicit institution of society" (Castoriadis 1991: 174). Institution, in this sense, is used as a verb and includes directly democratic creation without representation in legislation, jurisdiction, and law but also encompasses the totality of social institutions generally. The self-instituted society deliberately proposes to itself to fulfill common objectives and public endeavors and is the opposite of the closed society that is no longer critically self-reflective and becomes stagnant or self-destructive. We live in an era which includes self-destructive tendencies in which people lack empathy for one another, their surrounding environment, and the immediate future is painfully and existentially uncertain.

City & Citizen

The relationship between the city and the citizen—between society as a collective power and the individual—is critical. For how do people care for one another, themselves, and their surrounding environment if they are completely alienated from the creation of that society? In this book, Yavor highlights that citie s today "are run in a bureaucratic state-like manner that nurtures political and economic inequalities." Leveraging historical examples and theoretical insights, he argues that this has not always been the case and he insists that "a radically different approach is needed". He casts critical light on the modern relationship between city and citizen. Contrasting the problems of today's cities with democratic practices of citizens in ancient times is more than a theoretical exercise. It enables us to draw lessons from real world examples, past and present.

The ancient Athenian experience lasted for nearly two centuries. It is a rich source of information and lends itself to social-historical comparative analysis. Here, I'd like to extrapolate a bit further on certain themes; those contrasting our modern world with ancient times, to help elucidate the problems we face today in creating this new relationship.

2

Representation

The ancient Greek democratic forms contrast sharply with modern Western forms. As noted, in ancient times the relationship between society as a collective and power was critical. Democracy in its ancient form was direct whereas its modern form is representative. The significance of this difference, Castoriadis underscores, can be measured by noting that ancient Greek public law had no conception of representation and that the idea was unknown, whereas modern political systems enshrine representation in their very foundations. Occasionally, when people do seize power directly in the modern world, in popular assemblies and councils for instance, the seizure is a rupture in modern systems where the alienation from representation is, subsequently, exposed. The public assemblies of the global Occupy movements, for instance, illustrate this rupture, as the occupations opened spaces for public deliberation and reflection.

Exceptions in the ancient world include magistrates, who were elected based on expertise, such as military strategists (other magistrates were selected by lot or rotation), but it is important to note that among the polis all were considered to be equally knowledgeable about political affairs, that politics was a matter of doxa (common sense), and that representation was unnecessary. In contrast, in the modern world every politician is assumed to be an expert in some specialization and the citizen is expected to defer their decision-making abilities to the expert. However, this assumption is based on a deep tradition in Western political thought and ideology that is anti-democratic, in that it assumes that people are unable to govern themselves.

Until the early nineteenth century, the West held the authoritarian and totalitarian regimes of ancient Sparta in high esteem. But the rise of modern forms of representative democracy in the United States and Britain, as well as the newly established Greek state in 1830, enabled the reconfiguration of the West's political imaginary to better situate the more democratic ancient Athenian experience within its ancestral constellation as the supposed progenitor of today's democratic

3

systems (Cartledge 2009: 89–90). But there are fundamental differences between those aspects of the ancient directly democratic forms offering self-reflection for self-institution and those liberal representative forms of politics, which Castoriadis understood to be "liberal oligarchies" and thus not democratic in the deep, direct, autonomous sense. The ancient experience of democracy, however, predates the philosophical expression of liberalism as a body of thought and politics. Even so, the ancient experience stirred hatred among its contemporary critics who have supplied modern liberal oligarchies with philosophical reasoning for representative rule that dismisses popular self-governance.

One of the ancient critics to provide this reasoning was Plato, as exemplified by his dialogue translated into English as *Statesman*. This translation, however misleading, has enshrined a concept of representative rule into the Western Imaginary even though there was no state apparatus that was separate from the polis in ancient Athens, and the concept of "statesman" did not exist at the time. As translator David Ames Curtis noted (Castoriadis 2002: xxvii), it is not possible to accurately describe the person who participated in self-governing the polis as a "statesman." The Greek translation of this title as *Politikos* as well as the Latin translation as *Le Politique* are less suggestive. Nevertheless, this insertion of the statesman into the Western Imaginary has enabled Plato's antidemocratic message to be cemented into our conception of democracy as the rationalization for liberal oligarchy. That message included the argument that the statesman possesses true knowledge and that it is his task to prescribe to each individual who participates in society, each citizen, to follow what the statesman believes is the just thing to do. The underlying assumption being that the individuals who make up society are incapable of running their own lives (Castoriadis 2002: 32–3). This is complementary to modern democratic systems, where every politician is assumed to be an expert in some specialization, but it is also consistent with the basis for state socialist (bureaucratic capitalist) and totalitarian domination, from the factory floor to the public square. The statesmen know what is best. Castoriadis saw Plato as a great philosoph-

4

er but ultimately working to stop and suppress self-institution. Plato, in this sense, represented "everything reactionary and pro-establishment; everything opposed to the democratic movement ... found among the Romans, among the first Christians, during the Middle Ages, and in modern times" (Castoriadis 2002: 5).

Sovereignty

Ancient and modern social imaginary significations of democracy diverge on the relationship between people and political institutions as well. Castoriadis distinguished between the ancient awareness of the collectivity as the source of political institutions and modern sovereignty of the people from political institutions. For example, Castoriadis points out that Athenian laws always began with the preamble that "it appeared (it seemed) good to the Council and to the people, that ..." and in this way the collective source of the law is made explicit. It is rooted in the people themselves. In the modern West, however, sovereignty of the people has emerged (between 1776 and 1789) which proposes that political institutions are rooted in something other than the people, such as reason, natural law, rationality, or history (Karagiannis and Wagner 2013). For Athens in the fifth century BCE, the collectivity was seen as a set of individuals reared by the paideia (broadly meaning education) and the common works of the city, as noted by Pericles in his "Funeral Oration." Modern social contract theory, however, posits that the individual shapes society (i.e., Rawls's "Veil of Ignorance" [1971]). Whereas the objective of ancient political activity was to reinforce political collectivity, the modern objective of politics is to defend private, group, or class interests, including the interests of the state.

Rights and Political Participation

On the issue of political participation—where matters concerning private property and the family were considered beyond reach—the ancient Athenians excluded women, slaves, and migrants from political activity, while the modern

West has adopted universal human rights standards. These rights have come, however belabored, from protracted social struggles of the disenfranchised, such as the suffragettes who fought for the women's right to vote in public elections. Even so, many human rights—as individual rights but not collective rights—enshrined in law remain abstract aspirations as states are simultaneously responsible for upholding, promoting, and protecting human rights, while also being the violators of human rights. However, on the right of political participation, Castoriadis recognized the failure of ancient direct democracy to universalize and expand the right of citizenship to every person as the ultimate reason for its collapse.

Happiness, Mortality, and Immortality

Beyond political activity were the objectives of human activity more broadly. For example, Pericles described the way of living in and through the love of beauty and of wisdom. This objective was fulfilled through the paideia that the city offered. In contrast, the proclaimed modern objective is the pursuit of individual happiness and the sum of individual happiness, universal happiness, manifested through the acquisition of property, money, and power.

Castoriadis argued that behind this is a deeper difference between the stratums of ancient and modern social imaginaries which is the difference between mortality and immortality. Ancient mortality was closely associated with self-limitation, in that while one was alive they could commit hubris, or excess, and that this could tarnish their reputation. However, it was only when one was dead that they became free from the possibility of hubris and thus became happy. Immortality in the West, however, manifests itself in the modern ethos of indefinite progress, unlimited expansion, and rational mastery. These traits characterize most major cities in the West today.

Finally, the ancient Greek perception of mortality was rooted in an ontology found in the oppositions of chaos and cosmos and nature and law, which meant that it provided a sense of indeterminacy. This is the consequential difference between ancient and modern ontologies, whereas the modern ontology relies upon determinism, such as Cogito, ergo sum (Descartes). This deterministic ontology has its roots in Plato and has been expressed theologically in the Hebraic-Christian idea of a Promised Land which, Castoriadis proposes, ultimately transferred to the Western notion of "Progress."

Beyond Ancient and Modern

The purpose of this brief summary of differences between ancient and modern experiences is not to argue for a return to the ancient social-historical forms or its social imaginary. On the contrary, it is to elucidate these forms and their imaginary in order to deepen our understanding of autonomy and to enable a radical critique of the city. The point is to go further, beyond both the ancient Greeks and the moderns. More precisely, to instaturate (create original forms in their first instance) genuine democracy under contemporary conditions, to universalize the project of autonomy where each society faces their own unique set of *problématiques* (Wagner 2010: 53–60). For Castoriadis, this is only possible by demolishing the dominance of the economic sphere in the modern world (neoliberalism)—the heteronomous belief that capitalism is eternal and that markets know more than people—and by trying to create a new ethos connected at its center to humanity's essential mortality (Castoriadis 1993: 102–29).

Conclusion

As Yavor writes, this book is an urgent call for change of perspective, a perspective that puts people armed with radical imagination in charge of creating new citizens and new cities based on collective wisdom. While our present societies enable lives of hubris and the future is uncertain, there is also hope. Yavor outlines many positive examples, and these examples provide one feature for what I define as "Our decisive moment". In our book *Castoriadis and Autonomy in the 21st Century* (Bloomsbury, January 2021), co-authored with Alexandros Schismenos and Nikos Ioannou, I argue that this decisive moment is characterized by the combined weakening of liberal democracy, the rise of new ideological conflicts, the urgency of multifold planetary crises threatening nature and society, and new openings for the radical imagination. This decisive moment is a moment to choose between liberal democracy and the technical domination of nature, between state and capitalism or the emancipatory social movements of past and present—those struggling for autonomy, self-governance, and direct democracy. It is a choice between autonomy or barbarism.

Chris Spannos *is author of the forthcoming* Direct-action and autonomous organizing across the United Kingdom: London Solidarity *(Bloomsbury Academic) and a related forthcoming* Ken Weller Reader *(PM Press). He is co-author of* Castoriadis and Autonomy in the Twenty-first Century *(Bloomsbury Academic, 2021). He was formerly Media Editor in Oxford University Press' Higher Education division, Digital Editor for New Internationalist, Editor for ZCommunications, and Editor for teleSUR English. His writings have appeared in Le Monde diplomatique, ROAR and elsewhere.*

Introduction

*We should not kid ourselves: the climate catastrophe is
an epic war of the rich on the poor; corporate criminality on
a global scale.*
— ***Dimitrios Roussopoulos***[1]

The word "crisis" has dominated public discourse internationally for well over a decade and yet the solutions offered by institutions of the dominant system don't seem to deliver any type of substantial change.

After many years of political and economic crises that enforced austerity as the new global norm, the Covid-19 pandemic gradually exposed the material and imaginary consequences of this trajectory. In the face of a highly infectious disease that causes mass mortality, our societies were left with heavily crippled healthcare systems that faltered in the face of such a crisis. As if this wasn't bad enough, there also existed an institutional imaginary, the Social Darwinist idea expressed by officials at the highest positions of power that the old and the sick should be sacrificed in the name of economic prosperity. When measures were taken, they were far from enough. They repressed freedoms and channeled as few resources as possible to the needs of social healthcare. Neoliberal governments called for "individual responsibility," instead of a social one, suggesting that an individualist-based approach can work against a world-wide disaster. In short, as far as the ruling elites are concerned, business-as-usual must not be disturbed, even when the lives of millions are at stake.

The pandemic, however, didn't come from nowhere. It is a consequences of the unfolding ecological crisis. The way our societies have been exploiting nature has spearheaded existential threats such as climate change and deadly pandemics, resulting in the dire need of an organized response. But the most that the current system does in the face of this urgency is organize summits (most notable of which are the COP) between the global elites.

Hardly anyone expected anything meaningful or productive to come out of the most recent COP26. Even before the beginning of the summit, climate scientists such as Peter Kalmus, author of *Being the Change: Live Well and Spark a Climate Revolution*, warned that one of the summit's main goals—"Net Zero by 2050"—was a deeply flawed plan that provides cover for big oil and politicians to preserve the status quo.[2] During the days of COP26 activists deemed it a failure.[3] Even the very world leaders who organized it were skeptical from the beginning about the potential outcomes.[4] Moreover, when Global Witness looked through the list of participants, they found out that the fossil fuel industry, one of those most responsible for the climate crisis, has the largest delegation at the summit to ensure that its interests will be preserved.[5] Furthermore, historically speaking, the previous 25 COP assemblies have also led to no results. In short, from wherever you look at it, there was nothing to really expect but more of the same.

The main reason for the continuous failure of this approach is that it is led by the nation-state-capital complex, i.e., by extra-social structures that create and maintain a managerial class extremely prone to corruption and impunity. Even though national governments take power after elections, once in office they have the time, resources, and tools to entrench themselves in positions of authority and ensure their reelection. As philosopher Cornelius Castoriadis suggests, "once irrevocable representatives have been elected, their first and main concern is to secure their re-election."[6] Thus, it must not surprise us that decades of such summits between national governments, capitalist corporations, and technocrats have led to no results, while the ecological crisis deepens.

It is increasingly obvious that a radically different approach is needed, the exploration of which is the main goal of the current book. For some time now cities have been demanding to have more say over important issues.[7] This may offer a much-needed shift in perspective, because it brings the issue of ecological degradation closer to the grassroots. It is the majority of people worldwide that are suffering, and not the political and economic elites that have the luxury to hide themselves for a little longer before a catastrophe of some sort unavoidably reaches them. The privileges of those in positions of power are directly linked to the systemic exploitation of both society and nature, so it is more probable that they will prefer to gamble our future on extremely improbable technology that will allow them to continue down the same path, rather than dismantle the current system.

Cities today are run in a bureaucratic state-like manner that nurtures political and economic inequalities. But what I attempt to underline in the first section of this book is that, historically and theoretically speaking, this has not always been, nor must it always be the case. Unlike the centralized nature of the Nation-State, I argue, the city always contained a genuine democratic potential. From their inception until this very moment, cities have been revolving around two antagonistic cores. On the one hand, there were the temples of the powerful, from which empires and nation-states emerged; on the other, there was the public space (often in the form of public assemblies or local councils) that empowered, through deliberation and collective decision-making, the whole citizenry. It is the latter that contains the germs of a more meaningful and just response to our dead-end trajectory.

It is crucial to decolonize our minds from the grip of centuries of servitude and reimagine our life in common beyond the parameters of the Nation-State-Capital complex. Societies have once flourished in self-managed independent cities. Such democratic experiences still exist today, most notably in the Zapatista caracoles and the Rojava confederation, where democratic decision-making has allowed for feminist and ecological mindsets to flourish.

Instead of summits between national governments and multinational corporations, the time has come for transnational confederations that allow autonomous municipalities to coordinate their actions.

There can never be a guarantee that the "right" decisions will be made, but there are important aspects that might help immensely. In one such democratic setting, the countless citizen-led initiatives—driven by nothing else but the well-being of their communities—will have direct access to decision-making processes, instead of trying to influence politicians whose very privileged position depends on the exploitation of society and nature.

Here enters the goal of this book's second chapter: examining the preconditions for the emergence of a new anthropological type, based on genuine citizenship, that can be much more socially and environmentally responsible. By taking an active part in the management of its city, this citizen can take responsibility for the future of its community, as well as its natural environment, thus promoting a much-needed culture of citizen-stewardship. This is in stark contrast to the current passive, consumerist, and wasteful anthropological type.

The solutions offered by the powerful and the wealthy have repeatedly failed us. This book presents the urgent call for a change of perspective. It is time for cities and citizens to take centre stage in order for a meaningful and resourceful plan of action to be initiated. Anything less than this is simply a dangerous, life-threatening waste of time.

CITIES

Time to Reclaim the City

Change life! Change Society! These ideas lose completely
their meaning without producing an appropriate space.
— Henri Lefebvre[8]

The importance of the city nowadays is enormous since, as of 2007, the majority of the human population lives in urban spaces and the city's economic role is at its peak. As Antonio Negri suggests, "the city is itself a source of production: the organized, inhabited, and traversed territory has become a productive element just as worked land once was. Increasingly, the inhabitant of a metropolis is the true center of the world."[9] This is why urban spaces have been referred to over and over again in debates over political, economic, social, and other strategies for the future.

Modern urban landscapes are often depicted as "dark" places: as a place of alienation, of gray and repetitive architecture, with high suicide rates, expanding psychological disorders, and widespread metropolitan violence.[10] Cities are portrayed as prisons and its inhabitants as prisoners, deprived by the state and capital from the right to intervene in its creation and development. This is true for most contemporary cities. Urban landscapes are being redrawn, which can lead to the violent displacement of people from areas, whose value has risen, to others with lower value (such as the infamous *slums*).[11] This "game" is played with real human lives. Affordable housing gets displaced in order to facilitate capital and power accumulation. On the newly "cleared" lands emerge shopping malls, office spaces etc., all in the name of economic growth. Henri Lefebvre calls this type of city an oligarchy, managed for its inhabitants by an elite few state experts and corporate managers, thus ceasing to be a public space. [12]

The common people, who become victims in such "schemes," are powerless to resist these processes, at least through the officially recognized legal procedures—neither through the judicial system, nor through the so-called political representatives, all of whom are in positions of authority and thus intertwined with capital. So, amongst the grassroots are appearing different forms of resisting, reclaiming, and recreating urban public space. A colourful palette has emerged ranging from urban rioting, to self-organized market spaces for product exchange without intermediates, and neighborhood deliberative institutions (including assemblies, committees etc.).

The Loss of "Meaning"

One significant obstacle for people taking back their cities is the contemporary societal imaginary viewing, as Richard Sennett suggests, the public space as "meaningless."[13] Sennett points to the Nineteenth century, a period of rapid urbanization and economic growth, during which the outcome of the crisis of public culture was that people lost a sense of themselves as an active force, as a "public" (Sennett 1992, 261). Sennett suggests that during this period an important role in the process of depriving the public space from meaning was the adoption of more uniform dress and behavioral codes, more passive demeanor and less sociability, all of which can be seen as byproducts of the emerging consumerist culture and logic of representativity of that period. As Peter G. Goheen contends, "the street became the place for illusion rather than exposure to the truth."[14] In a sense, the public man was supplanted by the spectator who did not so much participate in the public life of the city as he observed it.

In order to overcome this point of view we need new significations to give back meaning to the public space. These can emerge only through practices of collectivities of citizens (i.e. the public), that would have positive and practical effects on the everyday life of society. Such processes already are taking place in the countryside and villages. Because of the crisis many are leaving the city life behind, returning to the villages that once housed their parents and grandparents.[15] In the countryside the city youth rediscover communal ways of life, sharing common resources, and learning traditional and ecological agricultural practices. But for the majority of those who undertake such steps, the village is an escape route from the uncertainty of the city, a form of escapism rather than part of political projects for social change.

As for those who remain in the cities, living under conditions of growing precarity, unemployment, and stress, the future does not seem so bright, with harsh austerity measures still on the horizon. This discontent is producing uprisings and mass mobilizations in urban areas, ranging from Istanbul's Gezi Park, Ferguson's uprisings against police brutality, the anti-World Cup riots in Brazilian cities, as well as the Occupy and Indignados movements in the squares of every major city around the world. In all of these cases, the question of urban planning is posed: can the city square remain the main cell of public deliberation, i.e., can it be simultaneously the *agora* (meeting and exchange point) and the basic decision-making body? Should a global festival of consumerism, such as the World Cup, have the right to reshape urban landscape, regardless of the human cost? Who should decide if an urban green space (such as Gezi Park) is to be covered with concrete and transformed completely?

For Cities of Interaction

There is a direct link between the above attempts of citizen intervention in the urban landscape and the broader project of direct democracy (i.e., broad public self-management beyond state and capital). In many of these uprisings and movements, the demands for participating in city planning and political decision-making in general were highly intertwined, because of the broad mistrust of authority and the rising interest in authentic democratic practices. According to Henri Lefebvre:

> *Revolution was long defined... in terms of a political change at the level of the state [and] the collective or state ownership of the means of production... Today such limited definitions will no longer suffice. The transformation of society presupposes a collective ownership and management of space founded on the permanent participation of "the interested parties" [i.e., the inhabitants or users of space].* [16]

The demand for broad public intervention in the creation and recreation of the urban landscape can easily be positioned at the heart of the project of direct democracy, since as David Harvey describes it, "The right to the city is... a collective rather than an individual right, since reinventing the city inevitably depends upon the exercise of a collective power over the processes of urbanization."[17]

Social movements consistently endeavor to intervene and reshape urban landscapes. In 2015, at the peak of the European migrant crisis, coalitions of solidarity groups and migrants in the city of Athens began establishing squats. One notable example was on Notara Street where different individuals decided not just to propose, but to practically initiate alternative solutions to the refugee crisis.[18] For years, arriving migrants were forced to seek shelter in open spaces such as parks and squares, where they were exposed to police violence and extreme weather.[19] What this group of activists decided to do was to reclaim their right to the city. They occupied an abandoned office building previously used by state bureaucracy and turned it into housing space for migrants. They accomplished this through democratic procedures: the building is, until this very day, managed through general assembly, open for Greek activists maintaining the space, as well as migrants living in it, and through various working groups. This very project is an example of the possibility of reshaping urban landscape according to human needs and desires.

During the same period similar things were taking place in the city of Manchester, where an empty office building was occupied by activists for housing rights and redesigned to accommodate unhoused people.[20] This was their answer to the housing crisis.

Another example is *guerilla gardening*, the act of people reclaiming unutilized urban space and turning it into botanical gardens in which they grow food.[21] The term *guerilla gardening* was used for the first time in the case of the Liz Chirsty Garden,[22] but as a practice, it can be traced back to the Diggers.[23] Nowadays such gardens exist in many cities around the world including London, New York, etc. Usually, the produce is distributed equally amongst the gardeners and their families in a democratic process. This very act of utilizing urban landscapes for the equitable distribution of food satisfies real human needs and directly opposes state bureaucracy and market profiteering.

Citizens have the right to manage their own urban environment, whether they do so by holding general assemblies in public squares or by adding switches to streetlamps to control urban light distribution.[24] However, citizens should have the right not only to place the city in service of physical human needs, but also to make cities reflect the very mindset of residents. Interactions between citizens should penetrate every sphere of urban space including the architecture, as was the case in the free city-states of medieval Italy where the citizens participated in urban planning through deliberative committees.[25]

In conclusion, we can say that the urban issue is becoming a central question today and the qualities of urban life are moving to the forefront of what contemporary protests are about. But in order for the city to acquire meaning as public space once again, citizens must be active members of the democracy, advocating for their rights and getting involved directly with urban management. Cornelius Castoriadis points to two stages in the pre-history of modern society in which such a public space was created: the Athenian *polis* and the medieval city-states.[26] We can also see the seeds of it in the Paris Commune, Barcelona of 1936–39, the New England Town Meetings, and many more. Only by linking the fight for citizen rights within the broader project of direct democracy, can the modern city become truly *public*, instead of a temple of economic growth, consumerism, alienation, and oligarchy.

Exploring Commons-Based Strategies for Urban Regeneration

To regain control over our cities, we need to reclaim our commons. The ascendancy of capitalism has steadily eroded public owner- ship and control over common resources and goods. To ensure an ecological future, we have to go in the opposite direction.
— *Eirik Eiglad*[27]

Day by day, State oppression turns into the new normal. Governments invested in widespread policing and the securit- ization of urban space create a vision of the city that contra- dicts the goals of autonomous movements.

The State, with its bureaucratic imaginary, envisions the city as a hierarchically organized, homogenous entity. This is in line with big-scale ideals of modernity, like the well-defined zoning of huge swaths of urban land that was so typical of the so-called socialist states. They were dominated by the idea of heightened demarcation: with neighbourhoods for workers' barracks where the workers slept, other neighborhoods with factories where labour occurred, neighbourhoods for leisure where they would go for a drink, and so on.

Although it is not so evident nowadays, such zoning is still here. There are, for example, neighborhoods reserved for the more well off, areas left for marginalized citizens, and then there are the trendy neighborhoods dedicated to the in- dustry of tourism.

When autonomous movements try to interact with the urban space, what they do directly opposes the State. They go against homogenization. So, the State tries to reconfigure tra- ditionally rebellious neighborhoods as trendy areas where one can go to drink a cooperatively crafted beer, smoke weed, or buy a St. Pauli T-shirt. Then you have these commons spaces that pop up and they suddenly offer a kindergarten service for the local community, as well as bookstores and other amenit- ies, becoming hubs for political organization. This defies the idea that a certain place should serve a single purpose.

These neighbourhood-based autonomous movements openly defy the vision of the rulers. In quiet neighbourhoods, intended to be mainly places where the workforce can get rest, such movements establish political assemblies where everyone can see what is going on, and start creating community centers. Citizens organize festivals. They create things that are not supposed to be there. They offer a radically different vision of the city. A revolutionary one, one supported by people like Bookchin and Jane Jacobs: a city where in every part of it you can find a mixture of activities. It's just like what the situationists suggested: a constantly changing and vibrant city.

The two conflicting visions of urban space today are (1) the top-down enforced homogenization and zoning of the city, and then (2) the possibility for citizens themselves to engage autonomously in cultivating their urban environment.

I disagree with the notion that the State functions like machinery, and can be driven towards the Left or towards the Right. Instead, I hold that the State is a certain bureaucratic mechanism that has a mind of its own. Rudolf Rocker said it a long time ago in his magnum opus *Nationalism and Culture*. He writes, "the machine [the Nation-State], because of the way it is built, can work only in a given direction, no matter who pulls its levers."[28] We have seen this all too many times, when radical left-wing parties take over the State but are unable to implement their initial agendas because the State machinery does not bend to their will. This led to rupture, for example, between Althusser and some of his students like Jacque Rancière, during the rebellious events of May 1968, when many concluded that every form of bureaucracy must be refused.

Technocrats tend to say that "the knife in the hands of the surgeon saves lives but in the hands of the criminal takes lives." This does not apply to the State. It has a specific structure. Its very design creates power discrepancies within societies. It operates like cancer cells. It expands itself. William S. Burroughs suggested that bureaucracy is always parasitic—a cell multiplying itself until it kills its host. He argues that,

> *A bureau takes root anywhere in the state, turns malignant like the Narcotic Bureau, and grows and grows, always re-*

> *producing more of its own kind, until it chokes the host if not controlled or excised. Bureaus cannot live without a host, being true parasitic organisms.* [29]

The State is a specific type of structure, which as a result of modernity and globalization, has copied itself all over the world. It tries to get into the heads of its opponents, penetrating antagonistic social movements and trying to reproduce there as well. This formalized bureaucratic ideal imposed by the State is gradually attempting to integrate the demands of different communities in struggle.

Commons-Spaces versus Other Spaces Created by Political Movements

Although we are used to identifying all types of liberated spaces under the same label—calling them either anarchist, autonomous, or whatever other name—the truth is that there is no single imaginary behind them. There are the more ideological and sectarian ones, which although managed horizontally without hierarchy among participants, maintain a political orientation that is not only indifferent to what's going on with society, but is even hostile towards the surrounding social environment. They tend to see society as a mass of conformists allied with the State. They unconsciously consume the propaganda of the State. The State tries to label such spaces as enemy of society and the former takes this role on themselves and starts seeing society in a hostile manner as well. This often comes as a result of their idea of ideological purity. They don't want to compromise on their ideas by mingling with local people who are not as well read or as radical as themselves.

On the other hand, there are other spaces that are viewed as commons that should belong to all people from a given neighborhood. People that participate in the creation of such commons-spaces (which may be in the form of social centers, squats, or occupied parks) often have a certain know-how, but their goal is not the making of what author Jonathan Matthew Smucker calls "shabby little activist clubhouses." [30]

Instead, they want to open their spaces up for wider communal participation. Such spaces are turned into something that is very much absent from the contemporary urban landscape: community hubs. Places where the community can interact. So, this is a very different approach. It is not a conspiratorial or closed group that operates its activities against the State. It is an effort by society itself to self-organize and create what municipalists call "urban villages."[31] This is why they are much more difficult to be rooted out by the government. There are often strong repercussions from local communities because they see themselves in these spaces.

Can Commons-Spaces Benefit from Particular Statist Responses?

Statist responses are usually a result from pressure exercised by social movements. So, when these movements are non-existent or in a very passive state, governments tend to strengthen their grip on society and increase the bureaucratization of everyday life. The emergence and activity of such movements work as a response to this bureaucratization (the expansion of the State in all fields). So as much as the State increases its attempts at complete control of society, there will also be resistance from below.

Of course, we have places like Eastern Europe where their experiences of authoritarian socialism and communism have created a monstrous cynicism and the repercussions are still being felt today. People there have fallen into a state of disbelief towards the possibility of change. When you have such a level of political cynicism, you descend into primal xenophobia, chauvinism, and collective narcissism. So instead of resisting the crawling bureaucratization of everyday life, citizens cannibalize each other. This is what we see today in Poland where huge swaths of society support the efforts of the State to ban abortion, which leaves Polish women to lead a heroic fight to retain autonomy over their own bodies. There are many other countries like Russia, Bulgaria, and Belarus where you see that governing oligarchies can do pretty much whatever they want and the populations take all their anger out on disempowered and marginalized communities like Roma, LGBTQ individuals, refugees, and more.

Social Movements as a Long-Term Sustainable Alternative

Autonomous movements must operate outside the State in order to, like Nietzsche would say, avoid turning themselves into monsters. Like in Greece, the introduction of certain legislation that allowed cooperatives to be formed more easily was introduced not because of any progressive politician, but because society itself acted and started exchanging products without intermediates etc. It was the autonomous activity of society that moved things towards that direction.

In Western Europe and in other countries, squatted spaces were legalized because of certain social struggles. This is much like the advent of human rights, which Castoriadis suggests were not introduced willingly by governments, rulers, or monarchs. Instead, it was the masses of disempowered people that resisted centralized and absolute authority, and as a result, those at the top were forced to make concessions on their hold on power. Moreover, universal suffrage was also once a revolutionary idea that the Levellers pushed forward. There is always this autonomous activity of society that is sometimes more subtle and sometimes more expressed through practice. But it is always this force that counterbalances the policies of the State and other forms of exploitation.

We must strengthen local self-governance and find ways to confederate such emancipatory localities. Municipalities are the only level of power where I think that some kind of community-oriented policy can be introduced, but they must always be directed by local self-governing structures like public assemblies. We need to learn from groups like Barcelona En Comu and Ahora Madrid, which tried to do something like this in major Spanish cities. However, their activity was much limited due to their choice to act through the structures of official municipal bureaucracies (local governments), which function like caricatures of the State. Their experience comes to show that the radical democratization of society cannot be channeled through bureaucratic, hierarchical mechanisms.

The other is that as participants in these autonomous movements, we must not see ourselves as avant-garde. Instead, it is of great importance to try to map the autonomous activities of society, to shed light on the different actors who do not necessarily consider themselves part of any movement, but whose activities still contrast the vision of the state. These individuals try to produce something completely different, something socially empowering and transformative.

One such mapping is not limited to mere observation, but also involves actively nurturing their transformative and revolutionary character. Not in the sense of taking over these activities and pinning a black and red banner on them, but to participate in them and to maintain their vibrancy as well.

It is very important to recognize how society counteracts the State and capitalism. We must also keep in mind that capitalism without the State is something impossible. We must abandon ideological purity and the idea that we can somehow develop a monolithic analysis which will remain untouched by time, space, and local contexts.

In short, the only way to make an alternative is to work beyond the State, because if the social movements and their struggles become entrapped within its imaginary and processes, they tend to be annihilated.

Lessons from the Commons-Spaces

As I said before, commons-spaces often become hubs for the creation of communal bonds. They produce a feeling of community and creativity within the urban space. It is like what Bookchin maintained in his book *Urbanization Without Cities*, that what we have today are not cities but sprawling urbanization which increased alienation and dissolution of old communal ties. What we see in the creation of communal spaces is the reestablishment of humane relations on a democratic foundation, resting on secularism and universal equality. There lies the crucial element. What we are offered as a

25

vision of the future from those that control the world today (i.e., the capitalist elites, the national governments, and the transnational technocratic structures that they create) is a vision of society fragmented into separate individual units which operate on their own, supervised by authorities beyond their control. Such a vision causes people to feel helpless and alienated.

We see this in the way current governments have framed the pandemic not only in Greece but in other countries as well. They speak solely of individual responsibility, while a pandemic is something that needs a systemic response. You cannot deal with a pandemic on the individual level alone. You either have the State as some sort of organized response or, as we have seen from the Zapatistas and the people of Rojava, there can be collective solutions that stem from the grassroots of society. There can be forms of non-statist, anti-capitalist democratic confederations. We cannot deal with a threat, such as global pandemic that spreads so rapidly within society, as mere individuals. The most unsuccessful examples unfortunately are the ones we see in the West, where the states refuse to step in because they see any investment in public health or mass testing as a waste of resources which they prefer to pour instead into the engines of infinite economic growth.

The City as Locus for Politics Beyond Statecraft

> [T]he rhetoric of Thatcher and of Reagan has changed nothing of
> importance (the change in formal ownership of a few large en-
> terprises does not essentially alter their relation to the State), . . .
> the bureaucratic structure of the large firm remains intact [and]
> half of the national product transits the public sector in one way
> or another (State, local governmental organizations, Social Se-
> curity);. . .
> — *Cornelius Castoriadis*[32]

Authoritarian Globalization and the State

For some time now, the globalized neoliberal system has
managed, in some respects, to stabilize and entrench itself
more firmly by taking explicitly anti-democratic and authoritarian forms. In contrast to the narrative offered by its supporters on the Right and chimed by most of its opponents on
the Left, neoliberalism's synthesis with representative democracy hasn't led us towards the dismantlement of state bureaucracies. Instead, it has resulted in their replication on
global, international scales (transgressing the national political discourse). The widely held notion of individual freedom is
a fallacy. Freedom is no longer free when it is accompanied by
the aggressive erosion of personal rights and the replacement
of individuality with consumerist atomization.

Despite all the talk of state "amputation," neoliberalism
instead proceeds in its reconceptualization. In fact, the state
apparatus is reduced to the role of central enforcer of capitalist dogmas and producer of anthropological types that are necessary to keep the current system going. Narratives of
"raging freedom" are invoked to mask the authoritarian
nature of the contemporary oligarchy. However, the State's
role as guardian of the neoliberal doctrine and its main pil-
lars, like unlimited economic growth, deepens its conflict with
society, often resorting to brute force, and thus becoming an
increasingly delegitimized entity.

In the face of this global authoritarian system, in which states seek to submit local populations to the will of international technocratic elites and transnational agreements (like TTIP), the far-Right and the large part of the far-Left seem to agree on the need to revive the independent nation-state. But their essentially bureaucratic proposal that is predisposed to racism seems to not find significant popular support, except for some sporadic electoral successes, provoked mainly by fear and insecurity, rather than political agreement. Examples from the age of national politics are reason enough for us to reject the retreat to the all-powerful and equally authoritarian nation-state sovereignty.

On the other hand, the proposal of the so-called political Center, both Right and Left, to stick to the current discourse is completely bankrupt. The dominant institutions of governance are completely delegitimized, with record levels of electoral abstention and rising social cynicism, thus forcing leaders to employ violence when facing popular disagreement and resistance. This reality leads many social movements and segments of society to explore new modes of organizing everyday life beyond the bureaucratic fragmentation enforced by the state.

In the last few years, the city has emerged as a potential contender to the nation-state. The radical geographer David Harvey has even argued that "rebel cities" will become a preferred site for revolutionary movements.[33] Great theoretical influence in this field is the work of libertarian thinker Murray Bookchin who, like the philosopher Cornelius Castoriadis,[34] returned to the forgotten ancient Athenian concept of the *polis*.[35] He attempted to reveal the revolutionary essence of this notion and its potential for our times. To quell parliamentary oligarchy, tribal nationalism, and capitalist relations, Bookchin proposed direct-democratic confederations of libertarian municipalities where citizens participate directly in local assemblies and elect revocable delegates to regional councils.[36] In the city and its historic rivalry with the State, he saw a possible public space where civic culture can shatter domination in all its forms.

Beyond Bureaucracy and Domination

The authoritarian nature of the contemporary system requires an anti-authoritarian paradigm if it is to be successfully challenged. While many have argued that the current rise in authoritarianism and technocracy is nothing but a temporary phase in the liberal oligarchic rule, others, like Walter Benjamin, have argued that the "state of exception" in which we live is in fact not the exception but the rule.[37] Electoral victories by far-right candidates and fascist parties are not some sort of systemic breakdown but are rather a continuation of traditional hierarchical rule by other means. Thus, it is up to all of us, all those "below," to bring about a real exception in the tradition of heteronomy and radically resist the domination of human over human and of humanity over nature.

The way this can be achieved is not through voting for political parties either on national or local levels, but through the self-organization and self-institution of society itself. This would imply communities organizing independently from established bureaucracies and determining their own agendas. It would be something like the demonstrations against the Dakota Access Pipeline where indigenous people and social movements managed to achieve significant victory, against both big capital and an alliance of state governments, in the preservation of their commons. These people built "from below" a movement that spread to more than 300 cities across the US and received solidarity from all over the world, including Thailand, Japan, and Europe.[38]

We saw in the last decade that popular resistances in urban areas have adopted an anti-authoritarian approach with democratic characteristics. Vanguardist structures like parties and syndicates, once dominant among social movements, have nowadays been abandoned and replaced by open participatory institutions. Demonstrations are increasingly turning to the reclamation of public spaces and buildings. These emerging resistant groups have effectively redefined democracy.

The role of social movements in these processes would be not to lead but to nurture these direct-democratic traits that stem from our very societies. Among the main questions for them should be how to successfully locate and maintain grassroots institutions that emerge in public squares and city neighborhoods in the short eruptions of civil disagreement with enforced policies "from above." And further, how their character could be transformed from purely symbolic to effective and decision-making. This also puts forward the need of regional and even transnational connectedness between such dispersed local grassroots institutions for them to be able to function sustainably in the face of state and capitalist hostility. For such germs of genuine direct democracy, we could also look beyond the contemporary Western world, in places like Chiapas, Rojava, and other indigenous communities, but also in historical political traditions that go as far as the ancient Athenian *polis*.

As Castoriadis suggested, we are at a crossroad in the roads of history.[39] Some of the more visible paths will keep us within heteronomy, in worlds dominated by the barbarism of international agreements and technocratic institutions, State apparatuses, and nationalist cannibalism. Although the characteristics of each one of them may differ, their foundational principle remains the same: that elites and predetermined truths should dominate society and nature. Humanity has been living within this framework for most of its recent history. The symptoms are painfully familiar to us all: loss of meaning, conformism, apathy, irresponsibility, the tightening grip of unlimited economic growth, pseudorational pseudomastery, consumption for the sake of consumption, technoscience that strengthens the domination of capitalist imaginary, and so on.

There is, however, another road that is not that visible, but is nonetheless present. Unlike the above-mentioned directions that are determined by extra-social sources, this one must be opened and laid through the political practice of all citizens and their will for freedom. It requires the abolition of bureaucratic fragmentation of everyday life, the reclamation of the public space and the *polis*, a reawakening of the creative imaginary, and re-articulation of the project of Autonomy. In the end, it is a matter of social and individual political choice which road our societies will take.

Beyond Statecraft Anti-Imperialism

*It is absolutely necessary to rebuild an intellectual and political
foundation for criticism and seeking change in the world, but
metropolitan anti-imperialism is totally unfit for this job. It has
absorbed subordinating imperialistic tendencies, and it is fraught
with eurocentrism and void of any true democratic content.*
— Yassin al-Haj Saleh[40]

Nowadays, narrow geopolitics and anti-imperialist discourses are often used as an ideological veil, which masks nationalist and authoritarian sentiments. This does not mean that imperialism is a thing of the past and we can only speak of it to hide more sinister reasons. It is more than evident that global superpowers still exercise hegemony over the rest of the world.

But there is a very specific problem in contemporary narrow anti-imperialism: it interprets politics only through the lens of relations between nation-state formations and excludes inner-social dynamics. In this line of thought, statecraft is often perceived as the only legitimate form, which must persist even at the cost of social oppression. The main question becomes the resistance to Western powers, more so than the establishment of any alternative social form. Often, we are served vague concepts of anti-capitalism and socialism, which doesn't surpass the nation-state and the paradigm of unlimited economic growth.

Authoritarian leaders and dictators are often more than happy to exploit this type of anti-imperialism and rally international support for their regimes. As Bookchin writes,

> *When "Third World" national liberation movements in
> colonial countries have made conventional avowals of socialism
> and then proceeded to establish highly centralized, often brutally
> authoritarian states, the Left often greeted them as effective
> struggles against imperialist enemies.... [D]espite the populist
> and often even anarchistic tendencies that gave rise to the
> European and American New Left, its essentially international
> focus was directed increasingly toward an uncritical support for
> "national liberation" struggles outside the Euro-American*

sphere, without regard for where these struggles were leading and the authoritarian nature of their leadership. [41]

Like classical ideologies, narrow geopolitical anti-imperialism continues to live in the epoch in which it initially developed. Many who share such views support Russia, China, or Iran as if they still live in the Cold War era and there is still an opposing communist bloc. Their anti-imperialist ideology makes them blind to the imperialist actions of the powers they support. As Gershom Gorenberg notes, "Russia's imperialist goal of extending its power into what were once Ottoman lands began before 1917, carried on in Soviet days with an ideological overlay, and continues today." [42] As an ideology, narrow anti-imperialism becomes a tool in the hands of nation-states, which seek to expand their influence and power. Castoriadis, when he suggests that "communism in its realized state... destroyed the workers' movement of other countries by subordinating that movement to Russia's imperialist policy," exemplifies how classical ideologies have been used to make popular movements serve imperialist goals. [43]

Its modernist fascination with large scales makes it explicitly state-centered doctrine. The only meaningful entities in the narrow anti-imperialist doctrine are hierarchical bureaucratic formations with national content. Thus, the world is interpreted as a battlefield between nation-states and their alliances. Every other social activity that moves beyond statecraft is either viewed as highly insignificant, due to its smaller size, or as a manipulation by another state formation. The structural architecture of contemporary societies is overlooked, or rather blindly accepted. Domination and growth are viewed as the main tools for the prosperity of geopolitical underdog nations.

It is understandable that in one such ideological construction there is no space for other projects which aim to undermine the foundational basis of state hierarchies. Often the attempts of local populations to self-organize through grassroots means (like popular assemblies), are met with hostility by certain left-wing tendencies, if they happen to threaten authoritarian, but supposedly anti-imperialist, governments.

One example can be found in the Arab Spring, where people in Northern Africa and the Middle East revolted against their authoritarian governments, organizing popular assemblies on public squares and in neighborhoods. We can suggest that in the imaginary of narrow anti-imperialism, local people and communities are too "tiny" and "insignificant" to act on their own, instead they are driven by the long and invisible hand of another stronger rival nation-state.[44] Also in this vein was the reaction of various "anti-imperialists" regarding the autonomous communities of Rojava and their stateless democratic experiment, which challenged the authoritarian rule of Assad in Syria.[45]

Syrian thinker Yassin al-Haj Saleh describes the Western-centered and dogmatic nature of contemporary narrow anti-imperialism in the following way: "a German, a Brit, or an American activist would argue with a Syrian over what is really happening in Syria. It looks like they know more about the cause than Syrians themselves. We are denied 'epistemological agency.'"[46]

Meredith Tax, in a review of Rohini Hensman's book *Indefensible*,[47] acknowledges this problem of scale when suggesting that,

> People in the Global South who seek democracy should be taken at their word rather than accused of being manipulated by the West, as if nobody else could possibly desire the same rights to free expression or assembly enjoyed by people in Europe and North America.[48]

Such thinking makes the current social organization inalterable. The only available choice is to align with one of the competing blocks (consisted exclusively of state formations) on the geopolitical field. This type of narrow anti-imperialism erodes any form of visionary thinking. Concepts like equality and freedom become emptied from content and instead are reduced to vapid slogans used by each of the sides.

Although many of these so called "anti-imperialists" call themselves internationalists, they often find themselves supporting nationalist movements, as they view national liberation as the main tool to weaken the regional control of imperialist powers. But as Bookchin observes, "the success of many 'national liberation' struggles has had the effect of creating politically independent statist regimes that are nonetheless as manipulable by the forces of international capitalism than were the old."[49] Often such regimes create a facade of self-determination and anti-imperialism for international use, while domestically nurturing xenophobia, chauvinism, nationalism, and even expansionism.

An example can be found in Milosevic's attempts to "cleanse" Muslims from Bosnia. Bookchin notes the following regressive elements in such national liberatory versions of anti-imperialism: religious fundamentalism in all its forms, traditional hatred of "foreigners," a "national unity" that overrides terrible internal social and economic inequities, a total disregard for human rights, often racism, and "ethnic cleansing."[50] He concludes that such struggles, which a generation ago may have been perceived by many western activists as "national liberation," end up as little more than social nightmares and decivilizing blights.[51] Such anti-imperialism carries the worst features of the very empires it claims to attack. They end up reproducing the same bureaucratic and lifeless machinery of the imperialists.

Once a regime has been established as a result of such national liberatory and anti-imperialist struggle, as history has shown so many times, it strives to strengthen its own power at the expense of neighbouring countries or even its own population. That's why social revolutions like the ongoing one in Northern Syria/Rojava, which tend to decentralize decision-making and empower all citizens, are met with hostility by anti-imperialists who root for Assad.

It must be clear that we should not oppose the strife of subjugated people to liberate themselves from a foreign yoke. We must be careful to not fall into the trap of supporting new, "domestic" imperialists in the place of the old "foreign" ones. Slogans such as "The enemy of my enemy is my friend" will most certainly not lead us towards genuine social emancipation. As Iranian journalist Rahman Bouzari suggests, "the first prerequisite of fighting imperialism is to fight the imperialist relations at home."[52] In other words, we should stand in solidarity with those struggles and uprisings that strive to abolish all forms of oppression. Those that fight against the exploitation prompted by capitalist growth and the hierarchies of nation-states and replace them with self-instituted forms of people power, where feminism, cooperation, and equality proliferate. Such projects often emerge in the form of self-managed municipalities that connect with each other in order to endure.

The two most notable contemporary examples in this direction include: the Democratic Confederation in Northern Syria, which set in motion a stateless, feminist and democratic revolution in the war-torn Middle East; and the Zapatista caracoles that have managed, for nearly three decades, to sustain an autonomously structured society based on direct democracy. It is the genuine revolutionary restructuring of political architecture that leads to social emancipation, and not the replacement of one ruling elite by another.

Municipalist Commoning and Factory Recuperation

Many still argue that the experience of recuperating workplaces is not an alternative to capitalism. And perhaps, in and of itself, it is not.... But it also goes beyond that: these same workers, rather than feeling depressed and having their dignity crushed, are instead leading the way for others to take back control over their own lives.

— Marina Sitrin[53]

For many years now the factory was (and continues to be) among the symbols held most dear by revolutionaries from all kinds of radical political traditions. Since the beginning of the industrial revolution, it has occupied the imaginary of social movements worldwide. With crises caused by the instability of capitalism and the centralization of statism, workers sometimes resort to the recuperation of their working place. This gives hope, but it also raises certain questions about the relation of factories to the broader society and even nature.

From recuperated factories in Latin America, like the legendary Zanon in Argentina, to European ones like the Greek Vio.Me., workers sometimes respond to crises by occupying this symbol of industrialism. Such actions are praised by radicals and leftists, but will they contribute to the colourful puzzle of collaborative and direct-democratic entities that can lay the foundations of a non-statist, anti-capitalist future? Or are they destined to remain entrapped within the imaginary of economism?

The Limits of "Workers' Control"

If such endeavors remain limited to the notion of "workers' control," there is a danger that this will create a gap that only a state apparatus can fill. Often it indicates that the function of workers' control would be to prevent the capitalists from organizing to sabotage production, to allow workers to get control over their profits and over the disposition of the product, and to set up a "school" of management for other workers. However, such factories remain isolated entities, playing the role of romantic symbols of bygone workerism that needs to be incorporated externally into some larger entity. As history has shown, this task is undertaken by vanguardist units, like parties, using such recuperations for the purpose of nationalization, thus strengthening "top-down" statism.

An example of this is the Russian revolution and the role of the Bolshevik party. The Bolsheviks—for whom the rebellious population was not ready for life in a stateless society—welcomed the workers control in the economic sphere in order to later incorporate it into the "all-seeing" state apparatus they built. The workers' self-management on the factory floor was later made an essential part of the Yugoslavian state. A more recent case is Venezuela under Chavez, where many workers resorted to taking control over their factories, just to demand later that they be nationalized, as they were unable to deal with the economic difficulties on their own.

Thus, the control of the workers over their working place, although essential, does not necessarily indicate steps towards liberation and deepening democratization. That's why demands and support for workers' control over factories can be found even among professional politicians and conventional left-wing parties. This does not mean that we should revoke any support for such endeavours, but we should remember that they are insufficient in themselves.

Municipalist Commoning and Recuperation

What can fill the void created by the workers control over the factories, is the paradigm of the commons. It suggests that resources of wide social significance can and should be managed by those affected by them. Often this implies broad social participation on municipal, or even confederal levels.

Factories are designed to be highly productive units. Their production reaches large numbers of households, and their functioning often leaves a serious imprint on the natural environment. Thus, the operation of factories can be considered as of common interest for the wider community, rather than that of the workers or the capitalists claiming ownership over them.

In this line of thought, factories should be managed by the wider social community, whose needs they can satisfy. In this way their incorporation into the statist economy or capitalist market could be avoided. This implies that the factories should be operated much like "consumer cooperatives," in which consumers participate in the management of certain enterprises. This does not mean that workers will not organize themselves on the factory floor, but that concerned consumers will be able to have a say and influence matters that concern them.

In practice this implies the creation of two sets of assemblies: (1) for workers and (2) for consumers. The workers' assemblies (one or more, depending on the size and number of operational departments of each factory) should be responsible for the direct management of the factory. All staff involved in the production process should have the right to participate equally and directly in the decision-making process concerning their enterprise. This assembly's decisions will have to carry the most weight, when deciding on the factory's production, since its members' very livelihood depends on it.

The second assembly type—that of the consumers—will involve people from communities that are using the factory's products. Their number should vary according to the population being served. The consumers' assemblies will have mainly consultative character regarding the quality of the production and the quantities needed by each community. In this way industrial manufacturers will be producing to satisfy real human needs that are publicly deliberated, rather than commercially imposed. However, consumers' assemblies should have certain "veto" rights over practices that could impact the natural environment and thus the health of nearby communities.

Ecological Dimensions

The idea of human domination over nature has resulted in the economistic mindset which separates human activity from nature's well-being. Thus, for many years the pollution of nature was overlooked in the name of unlimited economic growth, while communal environmental concerns were cast aside as symptoms of "backwardness," "ignorance," and even "selfishness." But our time is proving economism wrong. While contemporary capitalistic economies are constantly growing, human misery and inequality are proportionately rising, and the degradation of nature is threatening the very future of humanity.

The concern for nature should be incorporated in industrial production as well as in economic activity in general, which is responsible for a great deal of the ongoing pollution. By making production units produce for the satisfaction of actual human needs, many of them will no longer be needed. There is no need of a factory for every neighbourhood or even city, at least not in a non-capitalist setting. When producing for profit in an artificially commercial manner, a significant part of the production gets dumped away, because it can't be sold to generate profits, and is thus rendered "useless."

By maintaining the number of factories necessary for the satisfaction of real social needs, rather than using them for expanding the reach of capitalist economics, the paradigm of the commons could intertwine factory recuperation with degrowth. This implies that the factories located in close distance from each other, can coordinate with one another and with the wider local society in redirecting production, for duplication and competition to be avoided. In other words, factories can change what they are producing, if other entities are already producing the same products and are managing to cover the local demand. It becomes a question to be solved on a municipal or confederal level.

In an age of uncertainty and a deepening multi-layer crisis, it is surely exciting when people resist oppression by not just destroying, but by creating. Especially when they take over such industrial entities like the factory that has enormous productive capacities. But unlike deterministic approaches which view factory recuperation as progressive and revolutionary, we can see that this is simply not the case. It could also help enforce consumerism, bureaucracy, and "workerism" that could take regressive directions.

39

For the latter scenarios to be avoided, a serious rethinking is needed, one that will reconfigure the relations between work and leisure, production and consumption, and ultimately between economics and politics. A seemingly unbridgeable gap could be covered, giving new political dimensions to the contemporary struggles against injustice and exploitation.

Emancipated Neighborhoods within the Project of Direct Democracy

Cities have the capability of providing something for everybody,
only because, and only when, they are created by everybody.
— **Jane Jacobs**[54]

Cities have historically presented humanity with the space where people can establish life in common not on the basis of blood ties or tribal belonging, but on political agreement, solidarity, and mutual respect. They provided the environment where democratic politics could emerge and develop. Today, however, this space has been buried beneath suffocating layers of bureaucracy, on top of which is the homogenizing Nation-State. In this environment, everything essentially democratic is resisted by the dominant oligarchic institutions, while the logic of large scale and political centralization is presented as the only option.

The supporters of the current system—or even some of its opponents who have embraced the dominant imaginary—claim that there is nothing of political significance outside of parliaments, nation-state capitals, or transnational technocratic institutions. By thinking within these parameters, such logic cannot envision a democratic future. At most, it can think of public participation as a mere procedure—like plebiscites or public deliberations—that can be activated from time to time.

But direct democracy is much more than just a set of tools. It is a whole worldview and completely different form of social organization. The main difference between it and what we have today is where power is located. Today most of the authority is concentrated in institutions that are accessible to tiny segments of society. In a direct-democratic setting all power is dispersed among all people through interconnected grassroots institutions (public assemblies, municipal councils, etc.).

From this distinction, it becomes clear that one must abandon the current central political stage that promotes the logic of the nation-state and instead aim at the recreation of a genuine public space at the community level. Renowned American philosopher and political theorist John Dewey insists that democracy begins at the neighbourly community. [55] He links the development of democratic and participatory attitudes to local community discussions. Dewey advocates for the transformation of "every public school" into a "social center" where citizens meet to collectively solve problems. [56]

Castoriadis underlines that self-government requires,

> ... the greatest possible decentralization and the institution of grassroots political units on a scale where direct democracy could actually function in an effective way. Direct democracy does not signify democracy conducted by polling or over the telephone lines of television stations... but, rather, the participation of all citizens in the making of all important decisions, and implementation of those decisions, as well as the treatment of current affairs by committees of popularly elected delegates who can always be recalled.... The size of these grassroots political units should be of the order of, at most, 100,000 inhabitants (the dimension of an average city, a Paris ward, or an agricultural region of around twenty villages). Twenty or thirty of these units would be grouped together in second-level units. [57]

In this way power flows bottom-up, beginning at those levels closest to where we live, slowly moving to wider regional levels via confederal means that allow sovereignty to be retained at the grassroots level. Bookchin underlines this radically democratic dimension of confederalism, by calling for confederations not of nation-states (such as Yugoslavia and Czechoslovakia) but of municipalities and of the neighborhoods of giant megalopolitan areas as well as of towns and villages. [58]

It is in this line of thought that the emancipation of urban areas from the grip of bureaucracy is of crucial importance. When the inhabitants of a certain neighborhood or complex of buildings manage to institute a radically different mode of collective co-existence, then the self-managed units, of which Castoriadis speaks, begin to emerge.

First, in such cases a public space for the practice of authentic politics is opened: a spatial dimension that allows citizens to directly participate in the shaping and management of the institutions that maintain social life. The range of issues that each one of the inhabitants has to position and co-decide upon extends beyond the home (*oikos*) or the individual level. This creates the conditions for a radical democratic culture of freedom, responsibility, and solidarity.

Secondly, through such emancipated (and continuously emancipating) urban territories we get to see the practical application of the right to the city (as framed by Henri Lefebvre), which goes against the current dominant authoritarian tendencies that strive at subjugating our shared spaces to the doctrine of economic growth and capitalist speculation. The latter paradigm is continuously trying to turn entire areas into urban deserts—that is, areas deprived of neighborly relations, which serve narrow purposes like the needs of the tourist industrial machine. In such cases, as can be seen in areas of Athens and other cities around the world, the motive of profit-making is what determines the purpose of each piece of urban fabric. The communities that try to democratize their neighborhoods, on the other hand, can be seen as "spaces-as-thresholds" (to use Stavros Stavrides' term) that acquire a dubious, precarious, but also virus like existence. They become active catalysts in processes of re-appropriating the city as commons. [59]

It is important that the emancipation of urban territories rests on the following conditions which can ensure their long-term democratic functioning:

A) Instauration of grassroots decision-making bodies: the creation of institutions (like public assemblies) that allow all inhabitants from a given urban area to participate in its management. This provides the political means for an equal distribution of power among all community members. In the absence of such institutions, preconditions are created for the emergence of oligarchic attitudes that use a potential power vacuum to enforce their domination. If such institutions endure and manage to gain enough social recognition, then their legal recognition should be sought, in order to cement their status as the highest decision-making body at neighborhood level, thus replacing the dominant bureaucratic structures.

B) Connection with other struggles, movements, and communities: such experiments of urban emancipation must constantly seek to link their experience with other popular autonomous tendencies. In this way, they will not only use democratic processes in their day-to-day functioning but will also aim at instaurating direct democracy as a holistic political project for the radical transformation on a society-wide scale. Just as the gated communities of the super-rich are linked to the current mechanisms that advance the deepening of power discrepancies, so must the self-managed urban territories seek to connect to all these social efforts that fight for the inclusion of the greatest possible amount of people in the decision-making that determines the future of our societies.

C) Achieving recognition of a different type of housing: inhabitants undertaking directly the management of a given urban territory is the nucleus of a non-market, non-bureaucratic based system of residence. There is a real potential for housing that is determined by human needs and desires, a genuine Right to the City. It is of great importance that a legal framework is developed that keeps any given neighborhood or complex outside the rules of capital and statecraft, as was done by some of the examples below.

This is a general framework drawn from real-life experiences of the Right to the City. There are many examples in cities around the world where the residents have made bold steps towards the reclamation of their neighborhoods, infusing them with values of commoning, solidarity, and direct democracy. Here are but a few notable cases.

Milton Parc in Montreal[60]

The case of the neighbourhood Milton Parc, located at the heart of Montreal, is particularly relevant. In the 1970s its inhabitants began a struggle against a major speculator who bought a six-block area in the downtown of the city. The buyer wanted to demolish the whole area to build the so-called "city of the twenty-first century."

The inhabitants managed, over an eleven-year period of squatting, demonstrating, and holding information cam-

paigns, to save the neighborhood. But they not only preserved it—they managed to institute a radically different
model of self-management and housing that emerged amid
decades of struggle. They created the largest nonprofit cooperative housing project in North America, consisting of
642 housing units with over a thousand residents each acting
as democratic participants in the project. Now assemblies of
many hundreds of people decide upon the planning of their
environment, on the use of green spaces, on issues of traffic
circulation, on the quality of housing, and more. All of that
was made possible by the development of a sense of democratic citizenship and participation, as well as by the instauration of grassroots institutions.

Furthermore, the neighbors own the land in common.
There's no private ownership and therefore there's no speculation, making it impossible to buy and sell property within
the six-block area.

The community of Milton Parc has set an example of
what people power can do, but it did not stop there. They con
tinued pushing for emancipation of urban areas in their city
and abroad. They have established the Urban Ecology Center
in the heart of the Milton Parc area, through which they attempt to further develop and spread the ideas on which their
project is based. The community has also pushed the city administration to adopt the Montreal Charter of Rights and Re-
sponsibilities, which recognizes the human rights that citizens
have within their own city: rights in the area of housing,
transportation, democratic participation, water, culture, social activities, and environmental policies. Their achievement
that has now been celebrated by UNESCO. Since then, the
community of Milton Parc has worked with citizen initiatives
and local administrations in Mexico City, Gwangju, and other
cities throughout the world, to introduce such charters there
as well.

Acapatzingo in Mexico City[61]

Acapatzingo is a housing cooperative that consists of
eight hectares of homes and common spaces, inhabited by 596

resident families. Since the 1990s, an urban community in a self-built neighborhood in Mexico City struggled to obtain the resources necessary for the construction of their houses. They began with squatting the land, followed by marches, sit-ins, and other means for exercising pressure on the authorities, and eventually managed to buy it by the early 2000s and build permanent housing. Author Raúl Zibechi has called Acapatzingo "the best urban experience in Latin America."[62]

This neighborhood is managed through grassroots institutions of self-management. The inhabitants are organized into commissions and brigades that regulate the functioning of the community along the following lines: science, culture, and political training.

It was through such public deliberation and collective decision-making, that this urban community managed to install drainage, water, and electricity services. All these were set up and are since managed by the inhabitants themselves via commissions. Police are not allowed in the neighborhood, and instead a vigilance commission, controlled by the residents, looks after security.

Nowadays, the community of Acapatzingo is affiliated with the Organización Popular Francisco Villa de Izquierda Independiente (OPFVII). This organization has self-constructed nine other communities in which a total of 3,000 people live, all in the southeast of Mexico City. The OPFVII is distinct from most urban organizations in Mexico City in its absolute commitment to the organizational autonomy outside of the State. Thus, it is evident that the people of Acapatzingo are not only interested in the preservation of their neighborhood, but also in the replication of its self-management through the city and beyond.

Prosfygika in Athens[63]

The eight-building complex of Prosfygika, located in the center of the city of Athens, was built in 1933 for housing refugees from Asia Minor. With the passage of time, it became a vibrant neighbourhood with communal characteristics. Today, it is one of the biggest building complexes in the center of Athens, which has successfully resisted gentrification and has remained, to a significant degree, outside the reach of big investors and the State.

While some of its 228 apartments are still inhabited by descendants of the Asia Minor refugees, many of the emptied ones are occupied by squatters. Some of these new residents were political militants who decided to organize the neighborhood. In 2010 they initiated the Community of Squatted Prosfygika, having as its central decision-making political organ the Assembly of Squatted Prosfygika (SY.KA.PRO.)—a communal decision-making body for everyday life and political struggle.

Ten years later, the result of this initiative is that the project is a politically unified neighborhood. It contains numerous squatted apartments, autonomous communal structures like the Children House, Women's Cafe, and Bakery. It has a clothing workshop, as well as food and health structures covering the needs of dozens of people, many of whom are undocumented refugees.

The community constantly participates in social struggles and upholds a revolutionary perspective. On the local level they support political prisoners, student movements, and other squatted spaces. On an international level, people from the Prosfygika have travelled to support the social revolution of the Kurdish Freedom Movement known as "Rojava," where one of its members, Haukur Hilmarsson "Spark," became a martyr. It is this internationalist perspective and solidarity that allows the community to host Turkish and Kurdish revolutionary organizations and their political refugees within the structures of the neighborhood. They have also participated in solidarity campaigns abroad, with the most prominent example being Rigaer94 in Berlin.

Against Police Brutality: Towards Cities of Self-Limitation

*[T]he biggest enemy of society's security is the state
and the private organization's belonging to it.*
— Selma Irmak, member of the Democratic Society Congress [64]

Police arbitrariness and impunity are a common trait across cities of the world. In the U.S. the systemic repression, especially on people of colour, has provoked the outburst of many grassroots mobilizations and uprisings. A recent example is the brutal murdering of George Floyd on 25 May, 2020, by a police officer in broad daylight that shocked the world and sparked a wave of protests, demonstrations, and riots all over U.S. and abroad. In Greece, the killing of politicized youth has led to riots multiple times, the most significant being the December 2008 revolt that followed the death of fifteen-year-old Alexandros Grigoropolos by a policeman in Athens' city center. In more recent times, again in Greece's capital, the queer activist Zak Koustopoulos was first lynched publicly by a conservative mob, and then brutalized by the police units that arrived afterwards. He died from his injuries later that day. "Stop Police Brutality" has become a rallying cry in cities across the planet. Many have come to demand restrains and reforms, but further analysis shows that this violence has deeper roots and requires profound systemic change. In other words, the fight against police impunity is a matter of the society-wide distribution of power.

External Policing vs. Self-Limitation

Every society determines certain mechanisms through which its laws and rules will be respected and observed by all individual members. This assertion holds for the most tyrannical regimes to the most democratic ones. This does not mean that there is no difference between the various forms of law enforcement. On the contrary, the political structure of one society can be detected to a large degree, from the attitude its individual members have towards the dominant institutions and the way they are made to observe the common rules.

Castoriadis calls this enforcement of laws, roles, beliefs, ways of life, and so on, "limitation."[65] He distinguishes different types of prohibition according to the dominant political system. In oligarchic models (like parliamentarism and constitutional monarchies for example), where all the authority is concentrated in the hands of certain elites, this limitation seems external to the populace. People tend to defy it, because of the political alienation on which such oligarchic systems are based, thus potentially forcing the rulers to sometimes resort to more violent means. The fact that there is often talk about police violence in the liberal West signifies the oligarchic traits of the dominant system there, despite the efforts of the State to disguise itself as "representative democracy" (an oxymoron in terms), where the power supposedly lies in the hands of the people.

In direct-democratic societies, on the other hand, one observes what Castoriadis calls "self-limitation"—a process of collective creation and enforcement of laws. In such cases all members of society participate in social self-instituting and have the ability to control the enforcement of their democratically-derived decisions. But despite the general willingness of people to respect such policies and to not overpass them, there still are, and will be, cases of dissent. Here, self-limitation must still be imposed, otherwise the social integrity will degrade and collapse.

Despite our current epoch where police impose rules that are forged extra-socially—which is a form of police brutality in itself—the history of humanity is filled with practical examples of self-limitation that vary significantly from our common understanding of law enforcement. In fact, the idea of a professional police force, whose main task is to suppress mass eruptions of popular anger or efforts at regime change, is relatively new. There were significant periods when the enforcement of common laws and roles was left to citizens themselves, since their target was not to be imposed by a minority over the majority, but to ensure that collectively made decisions were respected by all members of the community. In such paradigms the target is not the suppression of mass disobedience or disrespect, but to simply maintain public order.

Ancient Greek Cities

The political differences between independent cities in Ancient Greece was evident from all spheres of social and individual life, including the ways in which each one enforced its laws and roles. The Athenian polis was the birthplace of democracy, where for the first time the notion of the "citizen" was introduced—a political subject that had the right to directly participate in the collective management of his city, alongside his fellow citizens. Despite certain serious shortcomings, many of which were products of the specific historic context, it allowed hundreds and even thousands of citizens to gather on regular assemblies and collectively deliberate on the self-institution of Athens. Sparta was on the other end of the political spectrum—a centralized militaristic oligarchy, where an elite managed the city, without the consent of the inhabitants.

In the case of ancient Athens, the maintenance of public order was delegated to publicly owned slaves (according to sources, these were of Scythian origin, and often armed with bows).[66] They were used to guard public meetings, maintain peace, and deal with people that have committed criminal offences. The investigation of crimes was left to the citizens themselves.

The fact that the most disempowered were delegated with this task—as strange as it may seem to most of our contemporaries—can be attributed to the democratic character of ancient Athens. With all citizens participating directly in the forging of the city laws and rules, there was the general idea that everyone could do the job of observing their implementation. Furthermore, since these slaves were public property, all the citizens had direct control over their actions and could prevent any abuse of power.

One shouldn't rush into judging the ancient Athenian polis for their shortcomings of slavery, or the absence of political rights for women. To begin, we must note that both slavery and the subjugation of women existed in almost all parts of the ancient world, while the notion of democracy did not. Secondly, the notion of slavery back then was much different from the forms it undertook in later historic periods.

According to Demostenes, slaves and free citizens were visually indistinguishable from one another, with the former often patronizing and outwitting the latter.[67]

On the other hand, in ancient Sparta, the maintenance of public order was among the duties of the Ephors, the highest Spartan decision-making body whose members were elected annually by all adult males.[68] They acted as judges in cases brought before them. The Ephors were also in charge of the Hippeis, a 300-member royal guard of honor who enforced the law. Among the other institutions of authority were the royal power and the House of the Elders.

This oligarchic type of social organization placed most of the political power in the hands of a tiny elite, like our current parliamentary system. This explains why the means of coercion were also in the elite's hands, ensuring its monopoly on power.

Medieval Times

In medieval England, law enforcement frequently changed its form due to many military conflicts. With its feudal and monarchic character, it is of little surprise that the means of coercion were under the control of the King or local magistrates. In rural areas and shires, law enforcement was delegated to the so-called reeves or sheriffs. They were subordinated to the royal power or local authorities and had as a main task to collect taxes, maintain order, and perform military service if needed. Lords, knights, and noblemen also had the role of policing the lands over which they ruled. This pyramidic structure favoured tax collection over everything else and allowed law enforcers to abuse their power at high rates, deepening power inequality in medieval England.

However, the political system was not the same around Europe during this time period. Many medieval towns became self-managed shelters for serfs and runaway slaves, and sought independence from feudal landholders and nobles. Such autonomous cities, that recalled the ancient Athenian polis, emerged in various places, most notably in Italy and France.

In the Eleventh and Twelfth century many towns in these countries became communes based on direct democracy and self-organization.[69] They didn't have professional police forces or royal guards, but local militias, made up of simple folk. These militias were subordinated to town meetings and councils, where citizens forged collectively the city's laws and roles. The high degree of social and political equality made the coexistence in these communes more harmonious. They had little need for numerous police forces, just like the ancient Athenians.

Shift Towards Crowd Control

The first crowd-controlling police forces appeared in the Nineteenth century, in order to serve the politically centralized purposes of the Nation-State and capitalism. The bureaucratization of society was reflected by mass suppression of civil organizing and creativity.

After a decree in 1829, the city of Paris, France created the so called *sergents de ville*, or "city sergeants," which were arguably the first uniformed policemen in the world. Similar formations appeared in England and the United States in only few decades—roughly from 1825 to 1855. These new police formations had nothing to do with a supposed increase in individual crime, but with the growing organizational activity among suppressed social circles like the workers strikes, urban riots, and slave insurrections.[70]

Paris Commune

An exception to this trend emerged from the popular insurrections that encompassed France's main urban center. The memory of the communes from the past remained alive for many oppressed populations and it comes as no surprise that when the people of Paris revolted in 1871, taking control over their city and repelling the local authorities, they named the new democratic organizational form the Commune.

With the new self-institution of Parisian society, a radical decentralization of political power took place, reshaping all spheres of public life. With local bureaucrats and police forces gone, the citizens had to create new ways of self-limitation to allow their communities to continue functioning. They began electing (and recalling, if needed) their own public safety officers, accountable to the neighborhood assemblies and councils that had elected them.[71] This never became a settled routine because the city was under constant military siege, but the communards did their best to keep the newly-established communal order as democratic as possible.

Total Militarization

Despite such short-lived moments of people power, the shift towards crowd control continued, slowly turning into a total militarization of urban space. With military conflicts transferring from international to city levels, the images of police forces battering down doors with tanks, armed with assault rifles, drones, and helicopters, became a usual thing for large metropolitan areas. Urban security forces have adopted military vocabulary and tactics.

This military colonization of urban life radically alters what happens to offenders who are persecuted by the police. As sociologist Jeffrey Monaghan writes, this trend "points towards a logic where enemies are to be destroyed and, when these enemies are demonized as subhuman or outside humanity, this destruction aims towards an apparent endgame: elimination."[72]

Police and Public Space

The contemporary system of domination uses police to prevent public spaces from becoming truly public. As Jacques Rancière put it with the famous phrase "Move along! There is nothing to see here," according to the law, there is nothing to do but move along.[73] It asserts that the space of circulating is nothing other than the space of circulation.

Politics, in contrast, work to transform this space into a dynamic realm wherein a citizen can participate in the self-institution of society. It refigures the space and its internal functions. Thus, bureaucracy must be challenged by political means.

The bureaucratic structure of contemporary police forces worldwide and their dependencies on states and private interests creates a permanent precondition for corruption among their ranks. This is evident from the fact that they are placed in the privileged position of being the "hand" of a dominant hierarchical order, which is not subject to citizen control. Thus, single units can exploit the law for their personal gains. As David Whitehouse suggests, "the law has many more provisions than [police] actually use, so their enforcement is always selective. That means that they are always profiling what part of the population to target and choosing which kinds of behavior they want to change."[74]

Unlike the policing role of communal militias, nowadays the ideological position among the police creates a caste with common interests which are tightly related to the maintenance of the current hierarchical order.

In order to put an end to police brutality and impunity, one cannot simply reform security forces. A radical change must take place on the level of the very foundations of our societies. This includes, first and foremost, the equal distribution of political and economic power among all citizens. This would allow citizens to directly, without intermediaries, reconfigure the societal organization and put an end to ongoing injustices. In this way the police, as an extra-social body that serves the interests of national governments and capitalist relations, will be abolished and replaced by conscious citizens that create their own laws and enact them.

Federations of Cities:
Castoriadis, Bookchin, AANES

A much more humane society is possible and desirable.
— ***Cornelius Castoriadis***[75]

Castoriadis insisted that what he envisioned as the project of autonomy—the project of a society in which all citizens have an equal, actual possibility of participating in the institution of society—is far from a utopian vision. On the contrary, he was convinced that it is possible, and "its realization depends only upon the lucid activity of individuals and peoples, upon their understanding, their will, their imagination." [76]

With this reasoning Castoriadis counters a specific line of thought that serves as a main argument in defense of the current oligarchic regimes—the question of scale. Rousseau writes in 1762 that a real democratic government requires, among other things, "a small state, where the people can assemble easily and where it's not hard for each citizen to know all the rest."[77] Although a lot of time has passed since the publication of *The Social Contract*, this argument, in one form or another, is still being used today in order to invoke the inevitability of parliamentarism. The conclusion of one such reasoning is that today there are only two feasible political systems. On the one hand there is some sort of totalitarianism, while on the other, there is representative oligarchy (wrongly named "representative democracy"). So, the closest we can get to freedom, this narrative suggests, is through the second option.

Castoriadis, however, throughout his works, challenges this line of thinking. He advances a third political model based on direct popular decision-making, what he calls "direct democracy." He suggests, that if we accept the dominant argument for the problem of scale, then we will end up with nothing but bureaucracy and the abuse of power. [78] Instead, Castoriadis insists that direct democracy is possible on the scale of millions, and even billions of people, when there are suitable organizational forms and structures that ensure the greatest possible participation of all.

It must be noted here that for the philosopher of autonomy, direct democracy cannot exist in an enclosed environment. According to Castoriadis, in the state of highly closed societies there is nothing that prepares the people "to challenge established institutions and significations (which, in this case, represent the principles and bearers of closure)." Furthermore, "everything is constituted therein so as to render impossible and unthinkable this sort of challenging."[79] Thus, there is a genuine need for the establishment of interconnected relations that transcend communal and social borders for the democratic values of constant interrogation and critical thinking to thrive.

The Federation of Councils

What he advances, of course, is not some sort of a giant assembly where all of Earth's population gather and deliberate, but a different, more appropriate type of what he calls "central power" that is effectively subjected to the people's ongoing control.[80] More specifically, Castoriadis speaks of the institution of a central (federal) assembly of councils, through which local councils and other grassroots decision-making bodies form a federation that is an expression of popular power, and not a mere representation of it.[81] In this way the problem of centralization is avoided, as the organs of local self-administration remain the sole bases of the central power, "which will exist only as a federation or regrouping of all the councils."[82]

Castoriadis' idea of democratic federation has little to do with what has come to be known as the State. The former gives the institutional framework for self-governing municipalities to coordinate with one another, while the latter subjugates all social spheres to one homogenous bureaucracy. A key difference between the two can be found in the underlining structure on which each one is based. For the State, this is the Parliament, where the general population elects representatives once every few years, vesting them with huge amounts of power. After election, the citizens are left with little recourse to effect the functioning of the elected body. The most society can do in such case is to either go out in the streets to protest or to vote for a different political party in the next election. As regarding the second option, Castoriadis underlines the fact that once in office, these irrevocable representatives will do everything in their power in order to ensure reelection. [83] This is one of the reasons why the phenomena of so called "political dynasties" dominating political life seems to be such a common occurrence in parliamentary regimes around the world.

In the federative system advanced by Castoriadis, there are no parliaments composed of irrevocable representatives. Instead, the underlining structure is what he calls the "central assembly of councils," attended by revocable delegates that are elected directly by the general assemblies of grassroots communities or larger geographical groupings. [84] These people can be revoked at any given time by the institutions that appointed them in the first place. Castoriadis suggests that this central assembly of councils will meet in plenary sessions, probably twice a week, or as deemed necessary. The delegates that consist of this organ, he continues, will have to give an account of their mandate (which will also have to be relatively short) to the grassroots institutions that have elected them. Castoriadis concludes that a compromise would have to be reached between two requirements. He maintains that, "as a working body, the central assembly of councils should not be too large, but on the other hand it must afford the most direct and most broadly-based representation of the people, areas, and organs of which it is the outcome." [85]

When comparing the two models, one can distinguish a major difference: on the one hand, the position of political representatives in a parliament is a position of power that lays beyond popular control. On the other hand, the delegate of a public assembly is not vested with any authority, but is tasked to transfer a decision or a proposal by his community to other communities that are part of the same federation, for which he is held constantly accountable and can be revoked.

In Castoriadis' vision, the delegates that attend federative organs would have only subsidiary powers pertaining to the execution of popularly made decisions and to current affairs.[86] The power lays in the hands of the general population and is exercised through different democratic tools that allow broad and direct participation. The cornerstone of this project of direct democracy are the grassroots political units, consisting of up to 100,000 inhabitants (the dimension of an average city, a metropolitan neighborhood, or an agricultural region of around 20 villages) where genuine self-management can be practiced.[87] It is on this level that the people will deliberate and decide upon policies that they want to be implemented. These decisions will then be presented and coordinated at the federal level by recallable delegates elected by these units.[88] Castoriadis insists that,

> At all those levels, the principle of direct democracy would have to reign: all decisions principally affecting populations at a certain level would have to be made by direct vote of the interested populations, after information [is circulated] and after deliberation.[89]

He also believes that in parallel to all these assemblies and councils, other tools like plebiscites can also be used for questions such as the adoption of federal law by the means of federal referendum.[90]

For Castoriadis, one such decentralized system has the potential to allow for the peaceful and harmonious co-existence of a mixture of diverse populations. He recognizes that in today's world there are identificatory passions and mutual myths that create divisive stereotypes and obstruct democratic participation.[91] On the other hand, in a "reasonable and pacified world," Castoriadis suggests, these populations will be organized in autonomous communes that will federate as they wish so that no incentive be given towards ethnic homogenizing by a bureaucratic structure like the Nation-State.[92]

Resolving the Antinomy of the Contemporary System

One important problem that Castoriadis detects in the way that contemporary societies are structured is that,

> Capitalist technology, and the whole allegedly rational organization of production that goes along with it, aims at transforming workers into passive objects, into pure executants of tasks

that are circumscribed, controlled, checked, and determined from
the outside—that is, by an apparatus that directs production. [93]

At the same time, he observes that society manages to function as long as "this transformation of workers into passive objects does not succeed."[94] The system functions because people don't follow all the bureaucratic rules to the letter. This is reminiscent of Graeber's suggestion that bureaucracies are utopian forms of organization since they are "organized in such a way as to guarantee that a significant proportion of actors will not be able to perform their tasks as expected."[95] In a way, there is a common recognition by both thinkers that the system is obliged to count on the very same people whom it strives to turn into machines. People are constantly excluded from all essential decision-making processes, but nonetheless societal functioning cannot rely on some initiative by the grassroots.

The overcoming of this antinomy, for Castoriadis, goes through the overthrow of the dominant form of organization by common people working collectively to undertake the direction of their activity. And since this antinomy is reproduced in all spheres of social activity, its resolution, according to him, is the collective management of social activities by the autonomous organs of those who participate, and most importantly, the establishment of federative relations between them. [96]

Bookchin's Libertarian Municipalism

Castoriadis is not alone in his support of the federative principle. The revolutionary tradition has many advocates. Pierre Joseph Proudhon is among the most notable. He claims that the federation's "essence is always to reserve more powers for the citizen than for the state, and for municipal and provincial authorities than for the central power, is the only thing that can set us on the right path."[97] Since his time, other thinkers have made significant contributions to the concept of federal alliance between free communities. Among them is Murray Bookchin, whose politics share many similarities with the political project advocated by Castoriadis, while their philosophies differ significantly.

For Bookchin, what he calls confederation is as equally important as self-sufficiency. What he means by this term is "the interlinking of communities with one another through recallable deputies mandated by municipal citizens' assemblies and whose sole functions are coordinative and administrative."[98] Just like Castoriadis, Bookchin views the confederation as a major alternative to the Nation-State. He seeks its historic expression in the American and French Revolutions, as well as in the Spanish Civil War of 1936.

In short, what he envisions are confederations not of nation-states but of *municipalities* and of the neighborhoods of giant megalopolitan areas as well as of towns and villages. In this setting, Bookchin suggests, the federative connections between communities will not be of informal character, but will be binding and municipal minorities might have to defer to the majority wishes of participating communities.[99] Traces of this logic can be found in Castoriadis' concept of *self-limitation*—the central element to his direct-democratic project—which indicates, among other things, the legislative authority society exercises over its members.[100] In other words, it signifies the creation of rules and regulations by a majority of the social whole, which bind everyone, even those who might disagree.

Bookchin emphasizes a crucial distinction that is intrinsic to federative organizational approaches, such as his project of libertarian municipalism—namely, the differentiation between policymaking and administration. In the democratic confederations envisioned by him, policies are decided upon by communal assemblies consisting of free citizens, while the administration of these decisions on a larger scale is performed by "confederal councils composed of mandated, recallable deputies of wards, towns, and villages." While local communities, in Bookchin's project, are autonomous, they are still exposed to wider society. According to him, if a group decides, for example, to violate certain human rights or permit ecological destruction, then the rest of confederated communities have every right to prevent such malfeasances through the confederal council. Libertarian Municipalism suggests that the assertion of a shared agreement by all to re-cognize civil rights and maintain the ecological integrity of a region is not something that is decided by central institutions (as is the case today), but "by the majority of the popular assemblies conceived as one large community that expresses its wishes through its confederal deputies."

In this way the process of policymaking remains firmly at the local level, while its administration lays in a trans-local, multi-communal one that overcomes isolationism and promotes interconnectedness and complexity, what Bookchin terms a *Community of Communities*. Castoriadis also underlines the importance of *reinforced agreements*—constitutional ones—in a direct-democratic federation. After being agreed upon, he suggests, their revision will be subjected to more procedures (such as more restrictive conditions, qu alified majorities, longer periods of reflection) before being able to alter them, so the integrity of individual liberties, rights, and rules, are guaranteed. In the end however, both thinkers agree that you can do so much in this direction. There is no magic solution that will guarantee that no mistakes will be made. Horrible acts have been committed by both monarchic and representative regimes. As Castoriadis suggests, "nothing or no one can protect humanity from its own folly."[101]

For Bookchin, the federative principle in its libertarian dimension causes growing tension with the nation-state that can be implemented in practice by grassroots organizational struggle and not by the *summits of the state*. Because of this he speaks of dual power: the instauration of networks between democratized municipalities delegitimizes the existing authority of statecraft. Such confederal links will not emerge overnight, Bookchin suggests, instead they can potentially follow after sporadic attempts of dispersed communities to increase their peoplepower. It is only when there already are such groupings that try to reclaim the control over their destiny, that they may come to the realization that some type of federative union is needed to overturn the current institutions of domination. It also implies that there are active social attempts to challenge the prejudices, habits, and sensibilities which nationalism and capitalism promote. In other words, these efforts seek to replace feelings like parochialism with a generous sense of cooperation and a caring sense of interdependence.

The Federalist Principle in Practice and the Case of AANES

Castoriadis sought examples for the implementation of the federalist principle in historic revolutionary experiences. One such was the French Revolution, in which the philosopher characteristically says that we see "a fantastic labor of explicit self-institution by society."[102] Within the processes that constituted this important historic experience, French society reinstituted itself based on local communities, among which a federation was established. According to Castoriadis, this federative element (that allowed for genuine self-governance), constituted the fecund period of the French Revolution and symbolized the irruption of self-instituting.[103] Unfortunately however, at a certain point, due to various unforeseen circumstances, the grassroots withdrew from the public space and allowed for elites to once again establish a heteronomous regime.

Let us now turn our attention to one contemporary example of a society where a direct-democratic confederation, reminiscent of Castoriadis' vision of a stateless federation, has been implemented in practice: the Autonomous Administration of Northeastern Syria, more widely known as Rojava. There, after a radical shift in the political orientation of the Kurdish Freedom movement, a new system has been implemented. The system is based on self-managed municipalities that coordinate with each other via federal processes which result in what has been termed Democratic Confederalism. Let us examine some of the similarities between this model and what Castoriadis has advocated.

The AANES system has at its grassroots level the Commune, which is the decision-making body of a living quarter (up to 350 families) of a city or a village.[104] Each such body establishes six committees—divided into educational, feminist, social, economic, peace, and self-defense subsets—that work on certain issues and present them to the communal plenary sessions. The Commune, although located at the very base of society, is considered the highest decision-making body. Since, as A.A, the chief administrator of the Movement for a Democratic Society, says, "the value of the commune's signature is more than the ministry's signature, as the minister cannot do anything if the commune does not approve it."

This grassroots decision-making body strongly resembles the self-governed units envisioned by Castoriadis. In both cases the highest authority lays at the base of society, where everyone can have access to it.

Several communes in a certain region gather in another place called the "People's House" (PH). Decisions that concern the territory in question are made at this level. People's Houses are also responsible for supervising the communes. In the canton Qamislo, part of the AANES, there are 97 communes who meet at seven People's Houses (Approximately one PH per 13 communes).[105]

At the communes there are also elections held to select delegates that serve at each city's council. These are bodies that deal with city-wide issues. From that level, people are sent to participate at canton-level institutions: the Legislative Assembly and Public Council. Each AANES canton consists of several cities. For example, there are 12 cities in the Jazira canton.[106] The approved laws in the cantons are filtered back in the communes, which means that the lowest levels are taking part in the macro level of decision-making, making it a bottom-up process. There is also a federal assembly for coordinating the cantons, which recalls what Castoriadis calls "central power."

Like the federative system advocated by Castoriadis, there are indications that delegates taking part in the different regional levels are revocable by their electorate.[107] In this way, grassroots control is exercised.

Unfortunately, such examples today are a very rare thing. Other than AANES and the autonomous caracoles (municipalities) of the Zapatistas,[108] there are hardly any other implementations of direct democracy on a social-wide scale. One of the reasons, according to Castoriadis, is because of,

> *The tremendous persistence of the imaginary of the Nation-State, which makes it seem that the peoples already constituted in States are in no way inclined to abandon "national sovereignty," while the other ones are especially preoccupied with the idea of achieving an "independent" state form, whatever its cost and whatever its content.* [109]

If this is the dominant imaginary condition of our societies, it will be difficult (but not impossible) to imagine a different type of social order—one based on federations of self-governed local units—that could lay the foundations of a truly democratic future.

The Temporalities of Climate Change: From Domination to Direct Democracy

[Being masters or possessors of nature] has no meaning—except to enslave society to an absurd project and to the structures of domination embodying that project.
— **Cornelius Castoriadis**[110]

The debates surrounding climate change almost always contain a certain urgency. It couldn't be any other way as it is an issue that, if unattended, will result in a catastrophe for humankind. So of course, we need well-coordinated action on a global scale to avoid the grimmest of projections.

This is where things get complicated. There are several approaches to rationalizing how one can initiate the much-needed steps to tackle climate change. The sense of urgency surrounding the issue plays a crucial role in the framing of our thinking.

There is a certain danger that arises when we translate this urgency into political projects, because it can easily be equated with the temporality of domination. See, centralized and bureaucratic structures are supposedly fast-acting as they are unburdened by mass deliberation. This, according to some, is what we need to face the climate crisis.

The Temporality of Domination and Bureaucracy

We can already see proposals in this line of thought coming to the fore of the climate change debate. Anatol Lieven in his book *Climate Change and the Nation State* claims the drastic action required to resolve this crisis can best be carried through the current governmental, fiscal, and military structures. [111] French climatologist François-Marie Bréon goes even further by suggesting that the fight against climate change goes contrary to individual freedoms and democracy, leaving us with no other option but some sort of "green" authoritarianism. [112]

This is the domain of the temporality of domination, where a fast-paced solution is introduced on short-term level.

Decisions made in bureaucratic and oligarchic settings function in an automated manner and are enforced on society. The real decision-making power is limited to a certain narrow section of the social whole or a specific mechanism (like the capitalist market or the state machinery), while most of the populace remains cut off.

While this faster pace is enforced on a short-term level, on a longer one we observe what philosopher Paolo Virno calls *déjà vu*. According to him, "[d]éjà vu arises when the past-form, applied to the present, is exchanged for a past-content, which the present will repeat with obsessive loyalty—that is to say, when a possible-present is exchanged for a real-past."[113] This is so because bureaucracy and domination replicate themselves and their structure in every chunk of space and time, to which they are given access. In other words, the political content of society is predetermined, and no structural change is allowed. Yes, there are reforms taking place at times (electoral spectacles are broadcasted live) but in this temporality the general structure is unalterable.

There is a serious problem with the temporality of *déjà vu*, as it tends to retain the very foundational basis that has led us to the current multidimensional ecological crisis—i.e., the imaginary of domination and hierarchy. As founder of social ecology Murray Bookchin advocated, "the notion that man must dominate nature emerges directly from the domination of man by man."[114] He maintained that social relations based on domination have gradually caused human societies to view nature and fellow human beings as a pool of resources waiting to be exploited.

Castoriadis points at the similar ways in which human beings and nature are exploited. He writes,

> For example, cities, a marvelous creation of the late Neolithic, are destroyed at the same pace as the Amazon forest, broken up into ghettos, residential suburbs, and office districts that are dead after 8 p.m. It is therefore not a matter of a bucolic defense of "nature" but, rather, of a struggle to safeguard human beings and their habitats. In my view, such safeguarding is incompatible with the maintenance of the existing system and it

*depends on a political reconstruction of society, which would
make it into a democracy in reality and not in words.* [115]

It is this interlinked exploitation that has led Bookchin to
conclude that "the real battleground on which the ecological
future of the planet will be decided is clearly a social one." [116]

The realization that social domination is directly interlinked with environmental exploitation has been more widely
accepted by an increasing part of the ecological movement.
But the urgency of climate change has been exploited by authoritarian policies that dominated alternative projects that
are developed by social movements around the world.

The Temporality of Direct Democracy

The direct-democratic alternatives that effectively up-
root every form of domination within society, as well as in our
relationship with nature, has a radically different temporality
from authoritarian ones.

First, since within the project of direct democracy every
form of bureaucracy and social hierarchy is abolished, public
affairs and issues (political, economic, cultural, and ecological) are collectively decided upon by all members of society.
Thus, people obtain more control over the pace of everyday
life, as they have the possibility to participate in the shaping of
its content. Author Kristin Ross exemplifies this trend through
her personal experience with the self-managed communities
that inhibited the autonomous ZAD in France:

> [T]he actual temporality of situations like the ZAD in-
> terests me enormously and is one of the reasons why I have re-
> turned there so frequently. Because I like the way time moves
> there. And what happens to time when you are not, say, working
> for a salary. Obviously, we are not talking about a situation that
> is entirely outside of the State, outside of capitalist temporality,
> but there is a way in which time moves differently, because
> salary labour has been pushed to the outskirts of peoples' life.
> And that means, that, for example, interruptions are different,
> or what counts as an interruption is different. Because people
> engage in a task and everybody works on a task and you are
> constantly interrupted by people who need something, or the

horses have escaped, so you have to stop what you are doing and catch the horses, and then someone comes over and says that we need a text right now about the demonstration in Nantes. And so, you stop and you write the text, but you see, none of that could happen if you were pushing a time-clock. So, the flow of time, the flow of peoples' pursuits is very different. [117]

As bureaucratic mechanisms like the capitalist market are no longer allowed to exploit and commodify everyday life, people can experience a radically different temporality that does not pressure nor oppress. It directly resembles the time of democratic deliberation exemplified by the Zapatistic principle of *command by obeying*. [118] The decision-making in the Zapatista municipalities is based on a process of consultation that constantly moves forward and backwards, which they express through the imagery of the snail and its spiral shell. [119] There are no bureaucrats, bosses, or profit-motives that put pressure on everyday life. It is reminiscent of the slogan "[popular] councils don't dance to the rhythm of the parliament!" which emerged during the German revolution of 1918–19. [120] Instead, democratic political architecture allows people to engage in deeper reflection and deliberation, creating preconditions for the creation of laws and norms that are decided upon by huge majorities. Therefore, society is much more inclined to willingly and consciously abide to such laws without the need of police enforcement.

The French Yellow Vests are yet another contemporary example of how genuinely participatory procedures tend to alter social temporality. By adopting a democratic confederalist structure the thousands of people that consisted this movement challenged the content of the week. [121] The contemporary system has determined that the role of the weekend is for the workforce to take a break from the pressure of work, which has consumed the rest of the week. There is obviously no space for genuine political activity in this time frame. The Yellow Vests proposed a radical alternative. They organized their demonstrations and general assemblies on those days that people were supposed to engage in passive consumerism, advancing in practice a temporality, in which political participation is more valuable than the passivity of economism.

The culture of direct participation that emerges within direct-democratic settings counters the *déjà vu* effect of bureaucracy and domination. With people *en mass* taking part in the management of public affairs, it creates preconditions for a temporality that is rich in political events. By opening politics to wide popular participation, social structures, institutions, and laws can be altered by society, unlike the enclosed character of oligarchic systems. In this sense, the temporality of direct democracy resembles that of a revolution, as it opens different future paths. In short, the former is a permanent revolutionary experience as it recognizes history as a human creation.

What Is to Be Done in the Age of Climate Change

Don't get me wrong, climate change is an urgent matter that requires action here and now, but if we agree that domination is its root-cause, then it is only logical to abandon every trace of it when exploring solutions. In this line of thought, we must remain vigilant regarding the efforts of authoritarian tendencies to pass bureaucratic measures under the guise of an "emergency." To allow elements of domination to pollute the alternative solutions advanced by social movements and communities around the world is to waste even more precious time, as we will be only scratching the surface of the problem, dealing with its symptoms, while leaving its root intact.

What is crucial is opening a genuine public space where the largest amount of people can directly participate in the development and implementation of solutions to the climate crisis. The solution here is not simply to find the fastest way to implement measures, as this often translates to authoritarianism. Instead, the goal is involving all citizens in developing and implementing coherent and well-thought solutions that will hold through time and will be widely accepted.

Author John Dryzek suggests the following features of wide public deliberations as potentially crucial for issues such as climate change. He maintains that,

> *It can generate coherence across the perspectives of actors concerned with different facets of complex issues. It can organize feedback on the condition of social-ecological systems into polit-*

69

ics. It can lead to the prioritization of public goods (such as eco-system integrity) and general interests over material self-interest. It may even expand the thinking of its participants to better encompass the interests of future generations, distant others, and non-human nature. [122]

If we do not take collective action against the very root of the climate crisis (namely, domination in all its forms) we are simply wasting more time and delaying the catastrophe. Castoriadis warns us that from experience we now know that,

> *The present-day (economic as well as scientific) tech-nobureaucracy is organically and structurally incapable of possessing the prudence required [to self-limit itself], for it exists and is moved only by the delirium of unlimited expansion.* [123]

Instead, he suggests that only a genuine democracy, one that instaurates the broadest possible processes of reflection and deliberation wherein citizens as a whole participate, can radically alter the current self-destructive path of humanity. [124]

The threat of climate change is too grave for us to continue thinking that we can work our way around it without revolutionary changes that will alter the very social fabric beyond capitalism and statecraft.

CITIZENS

Citizenship as an Inseparable Part of Revolutionary Politics

*To take no part in the running of the
community's affairs is to be either a beast or a god!*
— Aristotle [125]

When exploring social change, one must examine every aspect. Developing strategies and institutions that will help facilitate the development of a democratic and ecological society is of immense importance. So too is the anthropological type that will occupy it. In this latter aspect, the concept of citizenship plays crucial role.

Today, however, the term "citizen" has come to imply the belonging to a certain Nation-State and the right to vote once every several years for its governing elite. The far-right, proceeding from this understanding, has used it to discriminate against refugees and migrants.

Neoliberals, on the other hand, have advanced the idea of global citizenship detached from anything local. Lynette Shultz has defined this understanding by suggesting that, "a global citizen is someone who is a successful participant in a liberal economy driven by capitalism and technology." [126]

In the former understanding of citizenship, we have at hand a localist, semi-tribalist agenda, while in the latter there is a clear economistic one. Both deviate clearly from the essentially political nature of the origins of the term. "Citizen" and "city" share the same Greek root word—*Polis*. Citizenship means that you belong to a particular political community. In Ancient Greece it was the body of citizens that directly participated in the management of public affairs of their urban environment. Although immense shortcomings like the exclusion of women from the citizen body and the existence of slaves were in place, there is still something significant in this historic experience. It introduced for the first time a political framework of broad political participation based on passion for law-making, instead of power, blood ties, or knowledge.

Roots of Citizenship

For Aristotle, being a citizen was more than living in a particular place, sharing in economic activity, or being ruled under the same laws. According to him, citizenship was a kind of activity. He believed that, "the citizen in an unqualified sense is defined by no other thing so much as by sharing in decision and office."[127] The city was not simply a densely populated space, but a vibrant multitude of active agents. "Whoever is entitled to participate in an office involving deliberation or decision is," he thought, "a citizen in this city; and the city is the multitude of such persons that is adequate with a view to a self-sufficient life, to speak simply."

When Aristotle and his Greek contemporaries spoke of participation, they meant the direct participation of each citizen in the public assembly—not by voting for representatives—and willingly serve on juries (through sortition) to help uphold the laws. It was within this setting that the great ancient thinker concluded that "man is by nature a political animal,"[128] and that someone can be truly a "citizen above all in a democracy." [129]

Castoriadis points to the inseparable connection, which goes beyond mere localism, between citizenship and direct democracy, suggesting that,

> *Direct democracy certainly requires the physical presence of citizens in a given place when decisions have to be made. But this is not enough. It also requires that these citizens form an organic community, that they live if possible, in the same milieu, that they be familiar through their daily experience with the subject to be discussed and with the problems to be tackled.* [130]

Drawing on Ancient Athens, he underlines two basic traits of citizenship: *isgeoria*, the right for all equally to speak their minds, and *parrhesia*, the commitment for all to speak their minds concerning public affairs. [131]

Being a citizen was not merely a title, a privilege, or a passive identity. Castoriadis notes that it was all about education or *paideia*, which could not be obtained primarily from books and academic credits. In this sense, citizenship was a never-ending process based on active civic engagement. First and foremost, it meant becoming conscious that the *polis* is also oneself and that its fate also depends upon one's mind, behavior, and decisions. In other words, it was the very participation in political life.[132]

This was not an abstract form of engagement, but it emerged from a very specific space that nurtured such attitude—the public space in the form of general assembly (*ekkliseia tou dimou*) and administrative councils of delegates (often selected via sortition). Such democratic institutions created the conditions for a vibrant civic culture and a passion for politics which resulted in the rise of active citizenship.

In this setting there was no place for the pseudo-dilemma that plagues contemporary thought, that of the "individual" versus "society." The object of the institution of the *polis*, according to Pericles, is the creation of a certain anthropological type, the Athenian citizen. This person lives in and through the love and practice of beauty and wisdom, as well as the care and responsibility for the common good, the collectivity, the *polis*.[133] In short, the Athenian citizen was not a "private philosopher," nor a "private artist." He was above all a citizen for whom philosophy, art, and politics were ways of life.[134]

Citizenship and the Paris Commune

Citizenship as a revolutionary concept reemerged during the Paris Commune. It was, according to communard Gustave Lefrançais' account, during the public assemblies which emerged from the sections, that the people began addressing each other no longer as *mesdames et messieurs* (ladies and gentlemen), but as *citoyennes et citoyens* (female and male forms of citizen in French). This change shows a major transformation that happened on the social imaginary level and reflected the genuinely democratic essence of these grassroots institutions. If the address "mesdames et messieurs" stood for the saturated time of the nation, where nothing was allowed to change, then the words citoyennes and citoyens represented a people who had separated themselves from the national-statist body and instead opened a public space that nurtures bottom-up change.

The clubs and sections, that during the days of the Commune transformed into popular assemblies, provided the necessary space for people to act as citizens. According to communard Elise Reclus, these democratic institutions consisted of people "who, for the most part, had never talked to each other until then."[136] As they were open to all for participation, they nurtured this passion for political engagement and law-making, and this was actually a vital part of ancient Athenian citizenship. In this sense, as Kristin Ross notes, these institutions were "schools for the people," where participants educated themselves and developed civic culture.[137]

Citizenship and Ecological Stewardship

Citizenship, as it appeared in the above examples, must be understood as the direct connection between the individual and its social and natural environment. Furthermore, it implies a certain degree of responsibility that the former undertakes in respect to the latter. The citizen does not care only for herself, but also takes active part in the stewardship of her community, as well as her natural environment. Researcher Andrew Light suggests that "embracing the ecological dimensions of citizenship would be one way of fulfilling one's larger obligations to this thicker conception of citizenship."[138]

The direct participation that people can experience in the public spaces of citizenship potentially nurtures their interest in public affairs. In the same way, if they undertake directly the stewardship of their natural environment, then this will, quite possibly, develop a deepening ecological trait within civic culture. It could, in turn, raise their awareness of global phenomena like climate change, which the contemporary statist and capitalist elites neglect in the name of profit, provoking instead grassroots coordination in unseen proportions. Urban ecologist Steward T. A. Pickett, in this line of thought, suggests that "if the public bases its understanding of ecological processes on its local environment, then extracting ecological knowledge from urban systems has the best chance of enhancing ecological understanding worldwide."[139]

Beyond such hypotheses, however, this participatory understanding of citizenship strives at challenging the very root of the contemporary ecological crisis: domination. If people submerge in a civic culture of rational dialogue and cooperation on equal terms, then they will have to refute all together the logic of humans exploiting other humans, which gave rise to humanity exploiting nature. Because o f this ecological potential of citizenship, social ecologist Bookchin advances that,

> *The remaking of the constituents of republican represent-*
> *atives into citizens who participate in a direct democracy [...]*
> *can potentially eliminate the domination of human by human*
> *and thereby deal with those ecological problems whose growing*
> *magnitude threatens the existence of a biosphere than can sup-*
> *port advanced forms of life.* [140]

Citizen Education

The emergence of active citizenry which takes an active interest in public affairs and ecological stewardship depends, as noted above, on the creation and functioning of a proper public space that allows for direct participation. Such spaces serve as schools for citizenship.

This comes in opposition to elitist approaches that view broader engagement with collective societal decision-making as something that should follow an educational process that will be provided "from above," for example, by a progressive government. But there is a logical contradiction in such reasoning. Hegemonic rule does not teach people anything about self-governance; it only reinforces their habits of subservience and passivity.

Castoriadis underlines that there is only one way for people's opinions and judgements on political matters to be educated, and it is by letting them exercise political power, discuss, and make decisions. [141] In other words, the means cannot be contrary to the ends. If we aim at bringing into reality a direct democratic society, then getting people to actively participate from now is of key importance.

Thomas Jefferson, a very problematic and contradictory historic figure, advocated for a radically democratic ward-system, because of which Michael Hard suggests that his political thought belongs to the revolutionary tradition. He implied that the most important aspect of participatory democracy is how it changes people. According to him it has the potential to create citizens who will fight against any form of authority that tries to take power away from them. He writes,

> Where every man is a sharer in the direction of his ward-republic, or of some of the higher ones, and feels that he is a participator in the government of affairs, not merely at an election one day in the year, but every day; when there shall not be a man [...] who will not be a member of some one of its councils, great or small, he will the heart be torn out of his body sooner than his power be wrested from him by a Ceaser or a Bonaparte. [142]

Ultimately this understanding of citizenship is all about people coming together and collectively reclaiming power away from centralized entities like the Nation-State or an exploitative mechanism like the capitalist market. But it also implies an ongoing process of retaining power on the grassroots level, blocking the emergence of new forms of domination and hierarchy. In our contemporary context one such understanding of civic culture could provide communities with the tools to think and act beyond the limitations of economism and the social stratification of today's system. It most certainly has a crucial role to play in the reinstitution of a democratic and ecological society.

Citizens or Workers

When in countries that are called civilized, we see age going to the workhouse and youth to the gallows, something must be wrong in the system of government.
— ***Thomas Paine***[143]

For too long now many have been viewing social emancipation through an overtly economistic lens. This is evident from the persistence of some on insisting that class analysis is central to social change, exploring which economic class is most prone to revolt against its oppressors, trying to mobilize along class lines.

This is a by-product of the rise of what Karl Polanyi calls "economic society:" a Nineteenth century phenomena that is inseparable from the domination of capitalist markets that took place in the same period.[144] In this setting, according to Polanyi, the political and other spheres were subjugated to the economic sphere. Space was given to thinking and speaking that claimed universality and reduced human activity to the process of maintaining the production-consumption cycle.

When the project of social emancipation is subjugated to economism, its very goal shifts from empowering every single member of society with the power to participate in the management of all spheres of shared life, into a narrower struggle for better consumption conditions. This is not to say that the improvement of economic conditions is not important, but that it's far from enough. Even if radical changes are applied to the economy but the hierarchical political architecture of society remains unaltered, then sooner or later the inequalities advanced by the latter will create new economic elites. This was the case, for example, with socialism, where the bureaucratic/managerial class in charge of the State used its political power to take control over all other spheres of society.

Furthermore, focusing primarily on consumption and access to goods and services, as economism tends to do, can provoke scapegoating and social cannibalism. Disempowered groups may put the blame for their worsening economic situation on other marginalized and oppressed congregations, instead on the power discrepancies nurtured by the system. In this line of thought, Austrian author Franz Borkenau contends that it is easier to arouse nationalist feelings in the working class than feelings of international class solidarity, especially in periods of crisis and warfare, as the two world wars of the previous century so vividly reveal. [145]

Ultimately, the economic inequalities sparked by capitalism are not the only forms of oppression that torment our societies. Patriarchy (which is still a huge problem almost everywhere around the world) and gerontocracy (which today has taken the shape of technocracy), for example, provide much more ancient patterns of domination of certain social segments over others. Thus, social emancipation cannot be limited to this or that field alone.

Bookchin understood this very well and insisted that,

> *Workers have always been more than mere proletarians. Much as they have been concerned about factory issues, workers are also parents who are concerned about the future of their children, men and women who are concerned about their dignity, autonomy, and growth as human beings, neighbors who are concerned about their community, and empathetic people who were concerned with social justice, civic rights, and freedom. Today, in addition to these very noneconomic issues, they have every reason to be concerned about ecological problems, the rights of minorities and women, their own loss of political and social power, and the growth of the centralized state—problems that are not specific to a particular class and that cannot be resolved within the walls of factories.* [146]

This line of thinking does not exclude economics as such, but it refutes the narrowness of economism. It suggests that we cannot truly understand human societies through simply an economic lens. Castoriadis illustrates the need of a more holistic approach when analyzing the world by giving as an example hundreds of primitive hunter-gatherer societies, located in close proximity, with each one having different totems, taboos, matrimonial rules etc. [147] He insists that all these tremendous varieties of social collectivities and of types of institutions can by no means be explained by differences in the mode of production (as they were all hunter-gatherers). Such conclusions led Castoriadis in a totally different direction from Marx's rationalistic, economistic positivism.

What can help us move in the direction of a genuine social emancipation is not the passive belonging to a certain social stratum, be it economic or other, but the active stance and praxis in everyday life. Here comes the concept of citizenship, which Hannah Arendt suggests must be viewed as the process of active deliberation and the possibility of establishing forms of collective identity that can be acknowledged, tested, and transformed in a discursive and democratic fashion.[148] According to her, it's the sharing of power that comes from civic engagement and direct communal participation that can provide each citizen with a sense of political agency. There is today, however, no space for such attitude in the contemporary system of representation based on bureaucratic parties and state structures, because of which Arendt advocated for a more compatible one that will be rooted in the federation of councils through which citizens could effectively self manage political affairs.

This is a refusal of the role that the dominant system enforces on each and every one of us, i.e., belonging to a specific class with its own narrow behavioral patterns, and in its place a new one is advanced that broadens the horizon of collective action. It is what Jacques Rancière describes in his magnum opus *Nights of Labor*, where he examines how in the Nineteenth century, working folk refused their working-class temporality (heavy labor in the day with rest in the evenings), and instead claimed a different one that was supposed to be inhabited by aristocracy and bourgeoisie (instead of resting in the nights, they engaged in political debates, philosophical discussions, and poetry).[149]

By challenging the oppressive role that the system has predetermined for the working class, a path is open for the "humanization" of the latter, to use a phrase by Bookchin. He insisted that this depends on the ability of workers to undo their "workerness" and advance themselves beyond class consciousness and class interest to a community consciousness—as free citizens who alone can establish a future ethical, rational, and ecological society.[150]

In the end, you cannot envision a radically different world if your thinking remains entrapped in the categories of the old. As Castoriadis suggests, labouring people clearly cannot reach the point of "taking power" in the factory if they are not already envisaging in a certain fashion—be it obscure, half-conscious, or ambiguous—the question of power on the scale of society.[151]

In a setting of radical social emancipation, all people will undertake the management of all aspects of their life in common. Workers of different occupations, Bookchin suggests, would take their seats in popular assemblies not as workers—printers, plumbers, foundry workers, and the like, with special occupational interests to advance—but as citizens, whose overriding concern should be the general interest of the society in which they live.[152] Citizens would have to move beyond their current bureaucratically-enforced particularistic identity as workers, specialists, and individuals concerned primarily with their own interests. The project of direct democracy reshapes the content of municipal life as a school for the formation of citizens, with popular assemblies themselves functioning not only as permanent decision-making institutions but as arenas for educating the people in handling complex civic and regional affairs. According to Bookchin, it is the emergence of the new citizen that would mark a transcendence of the particularistic class from traditional socialism to the formation of a new anthropological type.

In such a direct-democratic setting social cohesion is not achieved through national or religious affinity, nor through certain economic interest. Instead, it can be attained by developing an all-encompassing political consciousness, through sharing and engaging in the practices and activities that make up a genuine public space and a framework of self-institution.

In conclusion, the question of liberating society from domination is not a matter that can be resolved by conditions that the system imposes on us, but on the active stances and attitudes we take. From citizen initiatives and autonomous zones in cities, to agricultural collectives and indigenous movements, germs of direct-democratic emancipation can be found in a diverse array of places. As Polanyi's concept of the countermovement implies, there is necessity in cross-communal alliances to achieve social progress. We will remain blind to them as long as we think within the parameters of the system and Nineteenth century dogmas. [153]

The Spatial Dimensions of Citizenship versus Mob Rule

The attraction of evil and crime for the mob mentality is nothing new. It has always been true that the mob will greet deeds of violence with admiring remark: it may be mean but it is very clever.
— *Hannah Arendt*[154]

Among opponents of direct democracy there is this re-occurring argument of it being prone to so-called "mob rule," as if people, once empowered, will probably turn into a mob.[155] This line of thinking, deeply submerged in the olig-archic imaginary, is highly fallacious and deceptive. There are certain reasons why people can degrade into a mob, and Hanna Arendt's work can provide clarity into distinguishing the former from the latter, as well as proposing alternative civic routes that can lead to the emergence of an active citizenry instead.

The Characteristics of the Mob

Arendt begins with stating that it is fundamentally wrong to regard the mob as a true reflection of the people, rather than its caricature.[156] It is only one possible formation of human beings, and not our supposed "inner-self" that waits to be unleashed. Arendt suggests that the mob, with its "enlarged tribal consciousness," more so resembles a "race," which is an extreme and totalitarian-leaning identity that the people can take.[157] As such, it is inherently attracted to violence. In this sense, we can suggest that the mob is anti-political, as it attempts to substitute power for strength.[158]

It is only logical then that the mob will search for and stand behind the "strong man," or the "great leader." This is quite different from another tendency that large swaths of people exhibited during all great revolutions: that of the fight for true, direct participation. If the second is an expression of genu-ine social life, then, according to Arendt, the former expresses the hate for society from which the mob feels excluded.[159]

The authoritarian tendency of mob mentality is enforced by a mixture of gullibility and cynicism, which has proven so effective for the rise of totalitarian movements. Arendt points at how,

> *Totalitarian mass leaders based their propaganda on the correct psychological assumption that, under such conditions, one could make people believe the most fantastic statements one day, and trust that if the next day they were given irrefutable proof of their falsehood, they would take refuge in cynicism; instead of deserting the leaders who had lied to them, they would protest that they had known all along that the statement was a lie and would admire the leaders for their superior tactical cleverness.* [160]

Ultimately, mob mentality is all about a thirst for authority. What unites all those who constitute mob-like movements is, for Arendt, the promise that each of its members will become such a lofty embodiment of some ideal if he would only join it. [161] She characterizes correctly such authoritarian tendencies as the underworld of the bourgeois class, where everyone is ready to exploit popular anger and desperation in order to get herself/himself into power. [162]

The Mob and the Plebiscite Republic

Nowadays we often hear of authoritarian leaders speaking of direct democracy when trying to underline their mass popularity. What they really mean, however, has nothing to do with any genuine form of democratic experience, as this would indicate the unmediated involvement of every single member of society in public affairs. Instead, Arendt suggests, they advance the procedure of plebiscites (or referendums), which is an old concept of politicians who rely upon the mob, as it rests upon people responding *en masse* to pre-formulated questions and then leaving those in power to implement their own interpretation of the result. [163]

The referendum is not a new addition to the political arsenal of authoritarian movements. Nineteenth century politician Paul Déroulède, one of the founders of the French nationalist Ligue des Patriotes, envisioned a "plebiscite republic" where the president would be elected by universal suffrage, and the popular will would be expressed through "legislative plebiscites."[164] In one such setting, at the core of the system is not direct popular deliberation, but the head of the nation, whose decisions, at times, are brought in a manipulative manner to the public for ratification.

In one such setting there is no genuine form of citizenship. Instead, we have a system based entirely on mob mentality, where an authoritarian movement, with an utmost devotion, elevates its leader, with the hope that each of its individual members will get a grip of at least a little bit of privilege over the rest of society. The usage of plebiscites in such cases comes as an ideological cover of a semi-totalitarian experiences and has nothing to do with democracy.

Beyond the Mob: Creating Spaces for Citizenship

The problem with our current political system, with its alienating and passive form of governance, is that it provides certain preconditions that are fit for mob development. Unfortunately, however, it does not elevate people into citizens—a vital element for direct democracy. Citizenship must be understood as the exact opposite of mob mentality. If mob mentality indicates the lowest human drive towards centralization of authority in the hands of a certain section of society, then citizenship is the sweeping distribution of power among all and the establishment of a political architecture of radical equality. It is an inseparable ingredient for freedom as a political phenomenon, whose roots can be traced back to the emergence of the Athenian *polis* and the first germs of direct democracy.

Arendt explains that the current regime of representative parliamentarism (today fallaciously dubbed representative "democracy"—an oxymoron) "could not save the people from lethargy and inattention to public business, since [it] provided a public space only for the representatives of the people, and not for the people themselves."[165]

In other words, apart from the ruling class, the rest of society has no access to the political processes that shape the direction their society is to take. One might object to this by pointing to electoral procedures that usually take place once every several years. They'll be reminded by the famous words of Jean-Jacques Rousseau that in such regimes people are free "only during the election of members of parliament." [166] In the end, there is a more than convincing correction to that thought offered by Castoriadis. According to him, the subjects of such regimes are not free even on election day, as their decisions have been prescribed by political parties, the propaganda industry, and other factors long before their visit to the ballot box. [167]

For Arendt, citizenship is something that is practiced and as such it requires a proper public space. [168] According to her, authoritarian tendencies emerge from settings such as the political environment of the West today, where a certain degree of liberty is given to people in their private capacity, but they are completely inhibited from participating as citizens. [169] In this sense, political participation is spatially limited, since it is not universally valid, but only becomes real when a majority of the people applies it. The active practice of citizenship by the people in the public affairs of their communities provides them not only with the experience of public freedom, but also with a sense of political and civic agency.

A suitable space where the people can act, and turn into, active citizens are the institutions of direct democracy, such as the popular council and the public assembly. For Arendt, councils are "the best instruments for breaking up the modern mass society, with its dangerous tendency toward the formation of pseudo-political mass movements." [170] Such popular democratic institutions are invaluable for the creation of vital citizenship as they are the only political organs where party membership plays no role whatsoever and are in fact spaces for people to act without intermediaries. It is for this reason, Arendt notes, that the councils of direct democracy will always conflict with parliaments as well as with "constituent assemblies," for the simple reason that the latter, even in their most extreme wings are still the children of the party system. [171]

Unlike others who, from fear of the rise of the excessive mob, seek to erect even more barriers to keep the masses from political power, Arendt concludes that "the only remedies against the misuse of public power by private individuals lie in the public realm itself."[172] In other words, the best solution to authoritarianism is the establishment of a political setting in which all members of society have an equal share in power and can collectively put limits on excessive and oligarchic attitudes.

Much time has passed since the publication of Arendt's *The Origins of Totalitarianism* in 1951, but the danger of authoritarianism is still present. The liberal oligarchic environment of the current representative regimes provides fertile ground for the emergence of mob-like tendencies that advance totalitarian projects and autarchic leaders. But such authoritarian movements are not an inevitable offshoot from public organization. Instead, they are a by-product of a system that denies the right to genuine political participation to the vast majority of society. It is this state of generalized disempowerment that drives the emergence of mobs. An antidote to such totalitarian tendencies is the creation of genuine public space, where a spatiality is provided for the emergence of another form of the people: that of the citizen. The exercise of citizenship, according to Arendt, is one of the best antidotes to authoritarian attitudes. It is only by means of direct political participation—that is, by engaging in common action and collective deliberation—that citizenship can be reaffirmed, and political agency effectively exercised.

From Pseudo-Rationalism to Rationality as Quality of Thought

> *We are no more nature rendered self-conscious than we are humanity rendered self-conscious. Reason may give us the capacity to play this role, but we and our society are still totally irrational indeed, we are cunningly dangerous to ourselves and all that lives around us.*
> — *Murray Bookchin*[173]

The dominant narrative of history tells a story of linear progress, in which humanity gradually becomes more reasonable and rational. We are travelling from ages of darkness toward the light. This tendency can be delayed, but cannot be stopped, or so the narrative goes.

The reality, however, seems much different. Our societies are in a trajectory towards self-destruction, regarding existential threats such as climate change. There seems to be very little rationality when it comes to the attitudes of the ruling elites to the climate crisis. One after another, their summits lead to nothing, while ridiculous tech-fixes are discussed in the name of an obviously irrational capitalist dogma that imagines unlimited economic growth as a possibility on a finite planet.

This very same narrative finds as reasonable also the advance of economism into all spheres of human life, a trend that produces time scarcity and bureaucratization of everyday life by commodifying human relations. Ultimately, it makes people more miserable and alienated.

There is, however, a growing amount of research that challenges the linear perception of progress towards ever-growing rationalism. Such research shows that, throughout human history, there has been a continuing clash between paradigms. In early cities, two antagonistic centers of power emerged—the public assembly on the one hand, and the temple on the other. The former attempted to empower an ever-growing amount of people (what we call direct democracy), while the latter gave birth to the rule by a small group of elites (what came to be known as oligarchy).

The latter managed to impose its dominance, not through rational debate and reasoning, but by the power of sheer force and deception. But despite that, the domination of elites met the resistance of the people in the face of popular uprisings and revolutions. Such were the French and the American revolutions, during which commoners began setting up institutions of popular self-management—which Hannah Arendt called the "Lost Treasure of the Revolution"—to challenge the rule of the few.[174]

Nowadays there are also existing examples where societies have rejected oligarchy and instaurated direct-democratic systems instead. The most notable of which are the Zapatista caracols and the Autonomous Administration of North-East Syria. In these cases, local populations rejected the exploitation of centralized governments and multinational corporations, and developed their own complex models of self-management that tend towards the inclusion of all in decision-making processes. Even when outside of such revolutionary environments, the people show much different priorities from the elites. One such example is the deliberative council on mobility that was initiated by the local government of the city of Bregenz, Austria.[175] It was attended by randomly selected citizens who were to propose visions and priorities for the future of traffic in the area. The proposal, developed by the council, focused heavily on the expansion of pedestrian walking, public transport, cycling, and public spaces. This was in stark contrast to what authorities and businesses envisioned, i.e., the investment in infrastructure that promotes car traffic and gentrification.

As we can see, this tension between oligarchic rule from above and the democratic aspirations from below are in a constant struggle. The supposed rationality of the former is often questioned, or outright challenged, by common people. The bureaucratic mechanisms and processes of today use reason and rationalism as an ideological veil with which to cover their exploitive and unjust nature. Often this leads to practices that threaten the very future of humanity, such as the ravaging of nature. That's why Castoriadis calls the contemporary system "pseudo-rational"—it claims to be based on rationality while acting irrational and unreasonable. [176]

Advocates of authoritarian modes of governance such as Slavoj Zizek, have suggested that a totalitarian-like state that will not "burden" people with political issues but will offer them instead a lot of free time to engage with things they supposedly wish to engage with. [177] The history, however, speaks to the exact opposite. Whenever the people have claimed their right to directly participate in the decision-making processes that determine the future of their community, there was an explosion of critical thought, creativity, and science. Most notable examples for this are the Ancient Athenian *polis* and the medieval Italian independent cities, both of which had their limitations and problems, but nonetheless allowed for mass civic culture to develop around participatory institutions and mechanisms like popular assemblies, citizen committees, councils of delegates, sortition, and so on. [178] These urban environments, where citizens organized life in common around political deliberation and agreement, allowed for rational thinking and reason to proliferate, as democratic processes provided the means for traditions and established "truths" to be scrutinized.

The rationality of the periods in question had nothing to do with the determinist rationalism advocated by the supporters of oligarchy. Instead, it characterized what Castoriadis called "the quest for truth." [179] He valued rationality not as a supposed linear progression, but as a quality of thought that always asks for justification and distinguishes between different forms of validity. [180] In this sense, rational thinking and reasoning have to do with processes of public deliberation, where opinions must be backed with logical arguments, and not with deception or coercion.

Unfortunately, this type of rationality is in retreat in our contemporary world. Instead, as Castoriadis suggests, the dominant pseudo-rationality puts an end to thinking and creation. [181] Bookchin, another thinker who valued reason as a quality of thought, underlines that today, "we and our society are still totally irrational indeed, we are cunningly dangerous to ourselves and all that lives around us."[182] He continues to suggest that "reason, which was expected to dispel the dark historic forces to which a presumably unknowing humanity had been captive, is now used to enhance the efficiency of domination."[183]

In order to overcome the current state of pseudo-rationalism and lead humanity to reason, Castoroadis believes we must cease adhering to a heteronomous institution of society and the internalization of the representations in which this institution is embodied.[184] According to him, this implies introducing a certain number of (not simply procedural) rules that render rational discussion possible.[185] In other words, for reason and rationality to have a place in our societies, radical changes have to take place.

First and foremost, this implies nothing less than a revolutionary reconfiguration of the political architecture of our societies. We must set up new institutions that will encourage public deliberation and mass participation in decision-making, so that space is given for dialogue to take place. In one such setting people will be allowed to move from infant-like national subjects and consumers into conscious citizens-stewards that take full responsibility for the trajectory of their social and natural environment. Public assemblies, participatory municipal councils and popular committees ca n provide the fertile ground for reason and rational thought to re-emerge. Otherwise, within the framework of the current system, there is simply no place for rationality. Everything is, instead, used to enhance and justify a completely unreasonable order that empowers a tiny percentage of the population, dooming the rest to a life of servitude and conformity. All social, natural and cognitive resources are used by the system to justify top-down bureaucratic rule.

Moving in a direct-democratic direction that will allow for rationality and reason to proliferate won't be an easy task. First and foremost, this is because the dominant pseudo-rationalism contaminates the imaginaries of many who come to oppose oligarchy. On the one hand, there is a large section of the Left that is deeply submerged in parliamentarism and economism. This group accepts the pseudo-rational linear determinism, which suggests that humanity is unavoidably moving towards increasingly larger scales that require further political centralization. As a result, they often come to blindly accept statecraft, labour as commodity, domination, and other systemic components of the status quo, instead of challenging them.

On the other hand, there is this troubling rise of conspiracy theories. Although these ways of thinking are critical of humanity's current state, they tend to offer analysis that undermines action and promotes cynicism instead. In the worldview of conspiracists, our societies have progressed so much that bureaucratization and technocracy have become all too powerful for people to initiate any genuine change. According to them, every event is part of a grand plan that is orchestrated by some secret society. Such worldviews often lead to a retreat from public affairs as adherents search for "deeper" esoteric meaning, so they can shelter themselves from the ills of the system. This is when, to use Bookchin's words, "the rational is replaced by the intuitional, and palpable social opponents are replaced by their shadows, to be exorcised by rituals, incantations, and magical gymnastics." [186]

Both trends take for granted the dominant determinist pseudo-rationalism. Instead of that, social movements fighting for social change should embrace rationality, not as an ideology of a linear progression, but as a quality of thought, which always seeks argumentation, reason, and justification. It's the type of rational thinking that will open paths toward different valid choices, instead of narrowly justifying what currently exists. A suitable setting for this is a social order based on the greatest possible citizen participation, where power is redistributed equally among all, and coercion is replaced by deliberation. Political architecture of this kind will have to be decentralized, with decision-making placed at the heart of where we all interact—in neighborhoods and in communities. For this decentralization to be sustained, without degrading into parochialism, confederal relations must be established between local self-managed units. As Bookchin suggests, "the confederation of municipalities, as a medium for interaction, collaboration, and mutual aid among its municipal components, provides the sole alternative to the powerful nation-state on the one hand and the parochial town or city on the other."[187]

The first steps towards something like that is the creation and maintenance of spaces where constructive dialogue can take place. Such spaces can be physical hubs like open assemblies and social centers, as well as digital platforms. The important thing is that the struggle for a direct-democratic society requires, as Harald Wolf reminds us, "a long and patient work of preparation."[188] The project of direct democracy, of which reason and rational deliberation will be an inseparable part, must be made appealing and desirable for a growing amount of people. This is a necessary step towards a popular revolutionary change that will overturn the oligarchic authority of the elites, opening up paths toward multiple alternatives.

Overcoming Individualist Passivity: Freedom as Political Action

Without action, all pleasure, all feeling, all knowledge is nothing but a postponed death.
— *Jakob Michael Reinhold Lenz*[189]

The conditions of oligarchy (rule by the few) not only fail to provide the spatial dimensions for people to practice politics and influence public affairs, but they also actively resist mass political involvement—what French philosopher Jacques Rancière has termed the *Hatred of Democracy*. In one such institutional setting, one can act only as an atomized individual, and not as a citizen that is actively and passionately involved in the collective management of society. Since our societies are structured around exclusively oligarchic lines—i.e., national-statist and capitalist ones—it is no wonder that there has been a diachronic retreat to various kinds of esoteric individualisms.

This trend is especially evident in times of crisis.[190] In conditions of war or economic hardship people are pressed by worsening living conditions, but the political architecture of their oligarchic societies does not provide them with the means of developing a collective response to the problem at hand. They can, and often do, seek collective solutions from outside the system, but the mainstream approach, heavily promoted by various systemic actors, is directed towards self-preserving attitudes. A characteristic motto of this atomized worldview can be found in the following lines by Samuel Smiles, the Nineteenth century "founding father" of the self-help genre: "heaven helps those who help themselves."

Philosopher Isaiah Berlin traces the emergence of a similar type of thinking back in Ancient Greece too, "when Alexander the Great began to destroy the city-states, and the Stoics and the Epicureans began to preach a new morality of personal salvation, which took the form of saying that politics was unimportant, civil life was unimportant."[191]

Oligarchies tend to inspire acquiescence with one's lot, insisting that there is nothing that can be done in the social realm. Thus, an exclusively individualistic perception of freedom is encouraged. This type of mindset can be defined by Berlin. "If you cannot obtain from the world that which you really desire," he writes, "you must teach yourself not to want it. If you cannot get what you want, you must teach yourself to want what you can get."[192]

Freedom becomes an individual affair, something that must be attained by everyone on his or her own. Becoming free is detached from political deliberation, and instead is equated with submission and passivity. This is arguably the mindset of every type of heteronomous society. Such is the case, for example, with religions such as Christianity, which discover, as Hannah Arendt suggests, "in free will a non-political freedom, which could be experienced in intercourse with oneself, and was therefore not dependent upon intercourse with the many."[193]

This understanding of freedom as a passive and atomized affair, one can argue, is a logical product of the oligarchic restriction of decision-making in the hands of narrow elites. But the very idea that one can be free in his "inner world," while he remains unfree in the social realm, is grossly fallacious. Freedom certainly implies the development of individual consciousness, unburdened by heteronomous dogmas and illusions, but it also prompts a radical decentralization of power and universal equality. Since the latter two are deeply political values, profound thinkers like Arendt have suggested that, "there is no actual freedom without politics; It simply could not exist."[194]

Being free, thus, must be understood as being politically active. It means that one has the possibility to participate in the creation and alteration of the rules and norms that frame our life in common. Of course, such political participation cannot take place within an oligarchy, since such a system's main feature is depoliticizing the great majority. Instead, it can only be realized in a directly-democratic project, based on a certain spatiality that allows for the exercise of genuine participatory politics.

It is in this line of thought that Arendt suggests, "that political freedom begins only in action... [It] is not 'inner freedom;' it cannot hide inside a person. It is dependent on a free people to grant it the space in which actions can appear, be seen, and be effective."[195] In a similar fashion, Castoriadis insists that "true politics, to the extent that these have ever existed, belong to praxis."[196]

No matter how much yoga one does, or how much self-help literature one reads, these can't really help one get hold of his or her destiny. At most, they can get her to acquiesce to her position, but she will never alter it. The same holds true for the freedoms offered by economically-centered systems such as capitalism. The latter suggests that it provides an economic freedom, i.e., being free to consume. While one can select among various products on a given shelf, without proper political freedom, one cannot challenge the short-term profit motive, economic growth doctrine, atomizing consumerism, or any other features of our modern system. Thus, it cannot really be called freedom at all.

Being free must be understood then, as being politically active in a specific type of democratic institutional setting. For Arendt, "human freedom is not merely a matter of metaphysics; it is a matter of fact, as are the automatic processes within and against which it always asserts itself."[197] Because of this, she suggests that "without a politically guaranteed public realm, freedom lacks the worldly space to make its appearance.[198]

There is a direct link between political action and the creation of suitable institutions. To act means to take an active part in the instituting processes of society. Only then can freedom be asserted. But it also implies that radical equality between participants is instituted, since the action of every person holds the same weight. In this line of thought Arendt underlines that,

> *In action, beginning and performance merge into each other, and, when applied to politics, this means that the person who takes the initiative and thus starts to lead must always move among those who join in to help him as his peers, and neither as a leader among his servants nor as a master among*

his apprentices or disciples. This is what Herodotus meant when he said that to be free was neither to rule nor to be ruled, and that therefore men could only be free in ισονομία, as democracy was originally called, in being among one's equal. [199]

Thus, the political architecture of freedom consists not only in the protection and security of the individual, but also his active engagement in the decision-making and instituting processes that frame the rules and norms of our life in common. In one such framework, the equality of the citizens, Castoriadis writes, is not only the passive equality before the law, as promoted by the proponents of liberalism, but also the active general participation in public affairs. [200] There are suitable institutions that have emerged in multiple historic moments, such as in Ancient Athens, the Paris Commune, the Spanish Civil War, the Hungarian Revolution, etc., that are based on and can further nurture political action. I refer here to institutional forms like general assemblies and popular councils that give space for broad public deliberation. Castoriadis describes this setting in the following manner:

> *Participation materializes in the* ekklesia, *in the Assembly of the people, which is the acting sovereign body. All citizens have the right to speak (isegoria), their votes carry the same weight (isopsephia), and they are under a moral obligation to speak their minds (parrhesia). Participation also materializes in the courts. There are no professional judges; virtually all courts are juries with their jurors chosen by lot.* [201]

In one such direct-democratic system there are no ready blueprints or premade solutions, only the space for political action. It is through action (individual as well as collective) that everyone in society can be free. Freedom is not the absence of restraints—something that could potentially lead to excessive behaviors and imposition of the stronger over the weaker—but the possibility of every member of society to equally participate in the management of their life in common.

Such freedom is not given, nor is it attainable on our own. It requires collective and coordinated action. It is social creation that requires passion as well as patience. All the modern short-cuts (such as self-help, esotericism, etc.) are tools that can give us the illusion of being free in an unfree world. Actual freedom is nothing short of genuinely democratic action.

Identities, Space, Time, and Emancipation

If we begin with the state, we end with the state. Let us begin instead with the popular reunions... the various associations and committees.
— Kristin Ross[202]

Political emancipation, in the most authentic and democratic sense of the term, means emancipation from the specialization of politics. In other words, it is a project of direct democracy where society—not some extra-social source—self-institutes its form and self-limits its activity. The seeds of such political emancipation can be traced to many historic moments. Among them are the Paris Commune, May 1968, but also the more recent one Zone à defender (zad). In all these cases we can see elements of direct democracy where politics is practiced "from below." We can also add, to a certain extent, the Yellow Vest movement with its recent adoption of a democratic confederalist organizational structure,[203] as well as its demands for more citizen participation.[204]

According to this understanding of political emancipation, there can't be a single socio-economic class or vanguard to initiate revolutionary change. For example, when author Kristin Ross examines the creation of genuine public space and time during the Paris Commune, she refutes the notion that the industrial proletariat were the sole actors of social change.[205] There was also, she notes, a significant role played by semiskilled peasants, who had migrated from the provinces to work in the city, as well as by traditional artisans, that were located at the bottom of the artistic hierarchy of the time. Prosper-Oliver Lissagaray reminds us that women were also present in the Paris Commune in a very dynamic way. He writes, "the women were the first to act. Those of 18th March, hardened by the siege—they had had a double ration of misery—did not wait for the men."[206] What was revolutionary during the Paris Commune was that each of these groups transgressed their bureaucratic roles and acted instead as citizens—as political beings capable of democratically determining their own future. Ross observed similar traits in May 1968, where she underlines the importance of other groups besides the students and the workers, including the peasants.

In both these cases the target of the popular rebellions was not only industrial capitalism, but the symbols of bureaucratization and policing of everyday life that stagnated spatiality and temporality. What was revolutionary about them was that people chose to transgress their heteronomously determined roles and acted instead as citizens, recreating a truly public space and time. Below I will examine three dimensions of political emancipation in this line of thought: the transgressions of bureaucratic roles and identities; the creation of public space; and the liberation of time.

Transgression of Bureaucratic Roles and Identities

One important characteristic of popular uprisings is the effort of those "below" to transgress their bureaucratically determined roles, imposed on them by state, religion, capital, and so on. For example, French philosopher Maurice Blanchot writes that the specific force of May 1968 derived from the fact that, "in this so called student action, students never acted as students, but as the revealers of a total crisis, as bearers of a power of rupture putting into question the regime, the State, the society."[207] This refusal reveals a general crisis of political representation and hierarchy, which cannot make people stick to their imposed narrow roles. These non-students, i.e., people who transgress their role, create a rupture with the dominant regime, putting into question the State and the current capitalist structure of society.

Similar traits can be observed in the Paris Commune as well. The communards attacked not only the monarchy, but all forms of hierarchy within French society. For a clear example of this Ross points at their choice to attack the Vendome Column (with Napoleon's statue at its top).[208] This column at Paris' center represented for Parisians the vertical structure of French society, and its destruction symbolized the destruction of hierarchy.

There were also similar traits in the individual attitudes of some of the communards. An important example is Napoleon Gaillard. Before the Paris Commune, he worked as a shoemaker, but after Parisians took over the city, he began making barricades on the city streets, which he viewed as a form of art.[209] Proof of this was his insistence to sign each of his barricades and take picture next to them, something which only people who were officially considered artists did prior to that. He transgressed several roles at once, which caused much distress to the likes of those who were hostile to the commune. One of those enemies was the poet Catulle Mendes, who was mourning not the drop in production, but rather his own anxiety which stemmed from this attack on identity. He worried what would happen "to a state if the shoemakers and the artists are not in their proper place."[210] Mendes was worried for not being able to identify, during the days of the commune, who was a worker and who an artist. This bureaucratic logic of narrow identity can be traced back to Plato, for whom in a well-constituted State a unique task is attributed to each person; a shoemaker is first of all someone who cannot also be a warrior.[211]

Similar conclusions are drawn by philosopher Jacques Rancière in his magnum opus *Nights of Labor*, where he observes that the greatest threat to the dominant order was when workers transgressed their roles as workers. According to him, when workers fought on the streets or sang revolutionary songs, they were still within their identity as workers.[212] It was when they stayed up late at night (a temporality supposedly available only to the higher classes who did not have to wake up early for work) and wrote poetry, philosophy etc., that they attempted to destroy the building blocks of the dominant order. They disrupted the strict bureaucratic roles and identities, opening up space and time for creative citizens who can collectively manage their society beyond capitalist and bureaucratic relations.

A more recent example can be found in the zad—the infamous anti-airport occupation of a piece of land in Notre-Dame-des-Landes, France that with time developed into an experiment in communal and direct-democratic coexistence.

It consisted of what Ross calls "a coalition of highly unlikely prot-agonists."[213] It was a colourful mixture of anarchists, trade uni-onists, local farmers (whose views could at times be even considered conservative), and many others. All these groups however, during the democratic experiences that emerged with-in the occupied space, transgressed their ideological or spatial identities and gave way to political emancipation that was char-acterized by active democratic participation and a sharing of re-sponsibilities. As Alex Kelly explains, "the complexity and richness of possibilities evidenced in these collaborations—when people at once defend and create together—are the very things we need to examine and work our way through."[214]

Creation of Public Space

The question of space is crucial to the development of emancipatory politics. In this respect, the French philosopher and sociologist Henri Lefebvre developed the concept of the right to the city: the collective reclamation of urban space.[215] The characteristics of this notion can be observed in many of the above-mentioned historic experiences, as well as in cur-rent movements and struggles.

During the Paris Commune, the urban space of Paris was transformed. The streets became not only spaces for transition, but also, as we saw earlier, into places for art. The sections, initially created by a decree sanctioned by King Louis XVI, become public assemblies that allowed for genuine public space.[216] Furthermore, the relationship between the city and the provinces was redefined with the communards is-suing a call for solidarity to all of France, and invited delega-tions from rural areas to Paris.

Such redefinition of space happened on the streets of Paris during May 1968 as well, but also in the farmlands of Larzac. A stark example of the creation of public space was the establishment of Worker-Student Action Committees that provided the environment needed for linking the university and the factories.[217] This space was very different from the bureaucratic trade-union life within factories where workers could run up against mundane procedures, control, surveillance, and maneuvers of all sorts. But it also differed significantly from academic life. It offered space for democratic participation that resulted in political emancipation. Like the committees of May 1968, the current Yellow Vests movement developed similar public space in the face of a network of popular assemblies that coordinated each other through confederal and democratic decision-making bodies.[218]

The experience of zad is especially topical regarding the question of space. First and foremost because local communities gave certain spaces value on the grassroots level, beyond the logic of bureaucracy and capitalist markets. The land on which zad took place was undervalued by state authorities and market mechanisms as "almost a desert."[219] The zadists gave much higher value to it, transforming it into a space worth defending.

Creation of Public Time

The question of time is crucial for political emancipation. Direct-democratic processes take movements. Its target is the creation of public time in which the past, present, and future are not predetermined heteronomously by authorities situated above society, but are formed through political deliberation, in which all people can participate.

During the Paris Commune, the choice of the communards to topple the Vendome Column was not only an attack on hierarchical verticality, but also an effort to liberate time. The effect this monument had on the temporality of the city was that it froze it. For the poet Catulle Mendes, the Vendome Column represented a determined time. He writes to the rebelling citizens: "It wasn't enough for you to have destroyed the present and compromised the future, you still want to annihilate the past."[220]

For Parisians, as long as the column stood above their heads, it signified the non-alterity of the future, the present and the past, i.e., a state of constant déjà vu. With its destruction, time was open to creative action. Nothing was predetermined; thus, the future was possible once again.

According to Jean-Franklin Narot, May 1968 had a temporality of its own, made up of sudden accelerations and immediate effects: mediations and delays had all disappeared. [221] Not only did time move faster than the frozen time of bureaucracies; it surpassed the slow, careful temporality that governs vertical strategy or calculation. When the effects of one's actions infinitely supersede one's expectations, or when a local initiative is met with impromptu echoes from a hundred different places all at once, space compresses and time goes faster.

Regarding the occupation of spaces by social movements like the Yellow Vests, Rancière suggests that,

> *Occupying also means creating a specific time: a time slowed down in relation to usual activity, and therefore a time removed from the usual order of things; but simultaneously a time accelerated by the dynamics of an activity that forces constant response to challenges for which people are not prepared.* [222]

In other words, the temporality of everyday life is liberated from the bureaucratic pressure of capitalist relations, but on a long-term social level, it is sped up as political change and creativity become possible. This double alteration of time changes the visibility of things and the sense of what can be achieved. Things that were passively suffered acquire a new visibility as injustice. As Rancière suggests,

> *When a collective of equals interrupts the normal course of time and begins to pull on a particular thread—today the tax on diesel, in the recent past university selection, pensions, or reform of employment law—the whole tight web of inequalities structuring the global order of a world governed by the law of profit begins to unravel.* [223]

Political emancipation is not simply the restructuring of certain social spheres or economic relations. Nor does it indicate the achievement of more rights by oppressed or marginalized groups, as it cannot be an individual endeavor. It is a holistic process that deconstructs all building blocks of the current Capital-Nation-State complex, replacing them with the basis of direct democracy. This process goes as deep as the replacement of capitalist/bureaucratic rhythms and zones with public space and time, as well as deconstruction of old bureaucratic roles/identities and creating new, much wider and holistic emancipatory ones in their place.

Sortition and the Public Assembly

Democracy arose from the idea that those who are equal in any respect are equal absolutely. All are alike free, therefore they claim that they are all equal absolutely... The next step is when the democrats, on the ground that they are equal, claim equal participation in everything.
— Aristotle[224]

In response to the deepening crisis of representation, direct democracy today comes up as an alternative proposal, put forward by the social movements arising worldwide. On the one hand, populists and party functionaries, in an attempt to attract the votes of the vast majority of people who are dissatisfied with the current state of affairs, have declared the semidirect democracy approach of the referendum as their solution to the current crisis.[225] The social movements themselves, on the other hand, through their own practices, have highlighted the direct democracy approach of networks of "face-to-face" assemblies. Discussions in political debates about reforming representative democracy in order to allow for broader citizen participation are becoming more frequent, while activists on the streets attempt to create autonomous structures beyond the state and Capital, which can potentially serve as groundwork for a fairer and more direct-democratic society.

Unfortunately, activists from different movements and the supporters of the aforementioned ideas often miss or even consciously neglect one practice in particular—choosing by lot (or sortition), originating in the Athenian *politia*, where the very concept of democracy is rooted. According to Aristotle, "choosing by lot is a sign of democracy while elections are a sign of oligarchy."[226] In Athenian Democracy, sortition, together with the institution of the general assembly, allowed the citizens "to rule and to be ruled."[227] The logic behind the sortition process originates from the idea, also arrived at by Lord Acton many centuries later, that "power corrupts." Most empirical evidence from their time to ours, points to this conclusion.[228] For that reason, when the time came to choose individuals that would be assigned empowering positions, the ancient Athenians often resorted to choosing by lot.

The supporters of direct democracy often have a complete and detailed vision of what a society managed by local assemblies and coordinated by federative councils on a regional level would look like. But when it comes to the question of how the members of these federative structures should be elected, often no satisfactory answer is presented. No matter how decentralized the structure of a society becomes, the danger of emergence of formal and informal hierarchies, undermining the democratic processes, is always present and the search for mechanisms for their prevention should be a concern of everyone if people want to keep direct democracy functioning. According to Michel Foucault, "power is everywhere and comes from everywhere."[229] In this line of thought, power is not limited only to one central structure (the State for example) or to the concentration of material goods in the hands of an elite. It is everywhere, reproducing itself in our relationships, language, and culture.

If we view this logic from an antiauthoritarian perspective we can conclude that the danger in a society based on direct citizen participation of elected delegates to become "professional politicians" (in the bad sense of the word) is very real. In many groups today, even ones that are part of the antiauthoritarian specter, unofficial hierarchies keep emerging and participants often do not have the means to confront these problems, which slowly corrodes the relationship between the activists and can even lead to the group's breakup. Choosing by lot is a mechanism precisely suited for dealing with that problem, preventing the establishment of strict "political" roles.

Another key aspect of sortition is that it promotes an active citizenry. In order to function properly, a direct democracy needs autonomous individuals, capable of critical thinking and interested in public affairs, or in other words: active citizens. Institutions, utilizing the mechanism of sortition, serve as universities on citizenship, where people immerse themselves deeply in the political life of the society for a certain period of time and acquire a sense of responsibility, and depending on the size of the community, all of them, or a large percentage of the population, pass through that process.

By knowing that they can be chosen at any moment, people are thus stimulated to act responsibly and to care about the common affairs of the society on a daily basis.

Sortition can also potentially help with the emancipation of women. While in a representative democracy (with elections as its main mechanism) governments are dominated primarily by men, in an institution where members are chosen by lottery, a society may decide for the configuration between men and women to be equal.[230] This also applies for marginalized communities. In general, during the electoral processes they almost always remain unrepresented, while in the case of sortition this can be regulated by the society itself.

Of course, thinking that sortition alone can prevent the emergence of demagogues and "professional politicians" is naïve. But if it's implemented together with short periods for holding the position, revocability and rotation, similar to the model that emerged in Ancient Athens, we get a comprehensive package of mechanisms that serves to prevent the occurrence of oligarchy.

It is important to note that while sortition can be a principal method for appointing most administrative roles in a direct-democratic society, some of them will still have to keep the electoral element. Some tasks demand expertise that most people lack, and because of that it is necessary that the citizens be able to choose between the experts they have. For example, in Ancient Athens, naval admirals and architects were chosen through elections, while sortition was the dominant way of choosing members of the Boule and magistrates.[231]

Today the process of sortition is not a widespread practice in governance. The most famous example is the Citizens' Assembly in British Columbia.[232] It offers empirical evidence on what choosing by lot can look like in practice, though in a non-direct democracy.

In 2003 the Local Government of British Columbia, Canada created a Civil Assembly chosen by lot and aimed at formulating a referendum proposal for a new electoral system for the local parliament. Until then the electoral system in British Columbia was standard, based on elections, whereby the winner formed the local government. Many residents, however, were unhappy with this model, feeling that their voice was not being heard. This led to the creation of the Citizens' Assembly for Electoral Reform, comprised of 160 delegates chosen by lot among all the inhabitants of the province—one man and one woman from each of the 79 electoral districts of British Colombia, plus two delegates from the indigenous communities.

The work of the Citizens' Assembly passed through three stages. From January to March 2004 delegates gathered every weekend in Vancouver to explore alternative electoral systems through an intensive series of lectures, seminars, and discussions. Each delegate received a fee of $150 for each weekend of work. In the second stage, the summer of 2004, delegates took part in a series of public hearings across the province to discuss alternative electoral models and to hear feedback. In the third stage, the autumn of 2004, the Civil Assembly met again every weekend for intensive discussions at the end of which delegates prepared a referendum proposal for a new electoral law. To the surprise of many, they did not choose a straightforward system of proportional representation, but rather what is known as the Single Transferable Vote system. [233]

In May 2005, the Assembly's proposal was submitted for voting. However, the referendum did not pass, because electoral activity was 57.3%, slightly below the required 60%. One reason is that this referendum was confined to the framework of representation, which in the past decade has been in a serious crisis that deepens with time. But this experiment gives us empirical evidence that we can use in the construction of other types of systems beyond representative democracy.

From all we have said until now it becomes clear that sortition is an organic part of direct democracy. It plays a dual role: it helps facilitate the daily administration of larger areas, while preventing the emergence of hierarchies. In itself, however, sortition is not enough, as demonstrated by the experience gained from the experiment in British Columbia. But in combination with the institution of the general assembly, like the politia of Ancient Athens, it helps build sustainable, democratic processes and active citizenship.

Sortition can be used in different contexts, as was shown in the aforementioned examples. Neglecting it at the expense of other institutions is a mistake, as it is a mistake to restrict direct democracy only to the so-called "political" area, as populists with pro-capitalist views are trying to convince us today. It is difficult to imagine how a group, a society or movement will operate in a truly democratic way if it does not use all the mechanisms of direct democracy, and instead chooses only some of them, replacing the rest with undemocratic ones. The fact that some direct-democratic institutions and mechanisms may produce negative side effects, which is a principal concern, does not mean that we should abandon them. Precisely through the implementation and experimentation with these types of institutions, structures, and mechanisms, we will be able to find weaknesses and correct them.

Educational Approaches towards Democratic Citizenry

Just think how the old traditional hierarchy is always trying to find out who is the best among us... and I think this is a bad idea. It is not the best, the greatest, but different that is beautiful. I don't want to see if someone is better or not better than me: I want to learn if something is different. That, from my point of the view is at the core of what we call democratic education.
— *Yaacov Hecht*[234]

Achieving comprehensive social change requires a radical alteration of everything. We often forget this and focus instead only on certain aspects of life, like the "fetishization" of the economy by most of the revolutionary movements. There are many reasons for this, one of which is education.

In our deeply economistic world, each one of us is viewed as a cog with specific tasks in a hierarchical mechanism. This is also reflected in large sections of the contemporary educational system. Specialization is introduced into one's life as early as possible. But as Castoriadis points out, this is extremely destructive to the personality of children.[235] With the rapid pace of technological development these days, this narrow specialization simply cannot keep up and new programs for adult re-education that are constantly being introduced. But to be able to absorb these new knowledges, Castoriadis continues, one must have a general educational grounding, and if this basis is maintained extremely narrowly through the process of early specialization, later education becomes impossible. Thus, a deepening crisis is formed in the educational field.

This crisis has been addressed by the same arguments used to excuse the need of the technocratic hierarchies determining the rest of society's spheres today. The narrative rests on the deterministic assumptions that an enlightened few can understand and thus lead the rest. The content and organizational structures of today's educational systems follow this logic and, as Ivan Illich puts it, they serve as "advertising agencies which make you believe that you need the society as it is."[236] The mystified world of technocratic knowledge demands obedient absorption of predetermined truths and thus there is little or no space for deliberation. According to Illich, "an individual with a schooled mind conceives the world as a pyramid of classified packages accessible only to those who carry the proper tags."[237] There are demands made by the "real-world" economy and educational institutions, along with the rest of society's activity which must produce the proper product (in the case of education: the proper employee/freelancer with the necessary knowledges) to satisfy them.

Things could, however, be rearranged in a completely different manner. There are alternative egalitarian and participatory forms appearing and already existing in other spheres of social life which could also be introduced in the field of education. The theoretician of democratic education, Hecht, calls the past and present predominant educational reality a "time of hierarchy," i.e., a state in which the student does what someone from above is dictating him to do, and thus no real knowledge is acquired. He calls for us to leave this state and enter a "time of knowledge," in which actual knowledge is developed through the deliberative networking of different and autonomous individuals.

Redefining Education

That said, we must rethink what today's societies consider education. The way it is currently instituted suggests that it essentially rests on a predetermined transfer of information that flows essentially from top to bottom. Thus, the imaginary it reproduces reflects the sources of this information.

There is, however, another concept of education: acts of cognition that criticize and negate this mechanical transference. If today's technology makes memorizing and preserving information immensely easier than ever before, then there is little or no need for humans to engage in this mechanistic process. Instead, it opens space for us to engage in what we are best at: imaginative creativity.

This emancipatory notion of education implies a levelling of the educational process. Information is first introduced to each individual for personal reflection. Then there is a collective, social level, on which these individuals collectively discuss and reflect upon it. This process of individual and social critical cognition produces knowledge that contains simultaneously the wisdom of the past with the boldness of the present. It also attempts to project this knowledge into the potential context of the future. Paulo Freire, author of *Pedagogy of the Oppressed*, insists on the importance of critical study (which requires dialogue and deliberation) in the production of knowledge. According to him, "when the reader critically achieves an understanding of the object that the author talks about, the reader knows the meaning of the text and becomes co-author of that meaning... The reader has worked and reworked the meaning of the text."[238]

The current search for educational improvement simply cannot be reduced to a renewal of the content being taught. Instead, new institutional forms should be introduced that resemble the notions of knowledge and learning described above. This will allow people to not only absorb information, but also to understand and develop the information further, becoming simultaneously accustomed to a dialectic civic culture that potentially could enrich the general public life.

The Public Assembly as Component of Education

One holistic approach to education implies that the organizational structure of such institutions to a large degree must resemble the content they strive to teach. This means that, as Yaacov Hecht points out, a school cannot teach democracy but remain undemocratic.[239] If we desire to create human beings that will be collaborative and autonomous, it will not be enough to tell him how to become so, but let him experience these principals and embrace them.

The public assembly is an institutional form that allows for such experience. It enables communities to acquire the capacity to manage their own affairs and to influence the educational process. The institution of assemblies in education, however, does not mean that the role of the teacher should be abolished, but rather that his authority should be replaced with more dialectic and supportive navigation.

If the introduction of public assemblies in educational institutions is to have any meaning, then they must replace the centralized decision-making bodies, currently in charge of schools and universities. Thus, their management, as well as the shaping of the learning process, will be achieved in a dialectic and deliberative manner between teachers, parents, students, and staff.

There are many advantages to the introduction of such participatory bodies. Among them are:

A) *Creating civic culture*
B) *Building well-argued opinions*
C) *Understanding and reshaping knowledge through deliberation*
D) *Encouraging responsibility-taking*
E) *Developing oratory skills*
F) *Resurrecting philosophy*

Such practices can liberate human creativity from the technocratic logic that restrains it and dominates our contemporary societies because decision-making is what distinguishes us from machines and mere objects. These practices will encourage our differences, laying the foundations of healthy political pluralism on which our society can thrive.

The educational potential of direct democracy is recognized also by practitioners of similar methods, like the cofounder of the Summerhill School in England, A.S. Neill, according to whom self-governance is "the most valuable asset in education and life," while the general assembly is "more important than all the textbooks in the world."[240] Yaacov Hecht, one of the founders of the democratic school in Hadera, Israel, stresses the importance of peer learning, calling for the creation of "classroom[s] where everyone teaches everyone."

The need for radical change in education is widely recognized. However, most of the attempts to reform it are limited, as Castoriadis notes, by the whole social framework, which deepens the current crisis. Every attempt to democratize the content being taught should be accompanied by democratization of the whole educational managerial structure, as well as of every other field of social life. In this way a truly public space could be opened by society itself that corresponds to its deliberated needs and desires. Otherwise, we risk continuing running around in circles, trying to fix the surface, while neglecting the rotten foundations that slowly erode the whole structure.

Time, Leisure, Work: Towards a Radical Transformation of Everyday Life

We have become a civilization based on work—not even "productive work" but work as an end and meaning in itself.
— *David Graeber*[241]

Free time has been, for some time now, undergoing a steady reduction. With the increasing spread of the gig economy worldwide, people find less and less time for leisure. Our jobs are steadily spilling beyond official working hours, invading the rest of our daily lives. As a result of this, an increasing amount of people feel overworked and exhausted. With more segments of free time being incorporated into the capitalist economy via the mechanisms of economic growth, we not only feel increasingly tired, but our very imaginations are getting dulled by the lack of temporal space for reflection beyond the economistic parameters of the system.

Although we have reached a technological level that allows us to drastically reduce the workday, one such perspective seems as distant as it ever was. Already, during World War I, Bertrand Russell suggests that modern technology greatly diminished the amount of labor required for the necessaries of life for all of society to be met. [242] According to him, in this period, despite the fact that huge amounts of people were employed in unproductive occupations such as war and propaganda, the techniques of the time made it possible to keep whole societies in fair comfort on a small part of working capacity.

Nowadays in many countries work has become automated and fewer people are employed to produce goods, but despite such preconditions for an increase of free time, there is the rise of what David Graeber calls "bullshit jobs:" the preoccupation of people with meaningless tasks that don't really lead to anything.

What one can see is a continuing trend in heteronomous societies (i.e., those based on hierarchies and exploitation) of time, both on individual and social level, being conquered by the logic of domination—as a result of which everyday life becomes fragmented, bureaucratic, and commodified.

According to Russell, historically speaking, spending one's time in the service of the ruling class was induced by the latter with a sense of duty.[243] It is supposedly one's obligation to engage in the routine tasks (jobs) that keep the system running, otherwise one might be labelled a "parasite." Who can forget the rhetoric of technocrats and world leaders regarding those EU countries that were most severely struck by the 2008 financial crisis. The latter were labelled pigs, because they were supposedly too lazy (although no facts indicated such thing), and thus guilty for the crash of their economies.

One can also think of the famous aphorism "he who does not work, neither shall he eat" that first appears in the New Testament and is later quoted even by Lenin in his 1917 work, *The State and Revolution*. In theocracies, exploitative capitalist regimes, or even socialist countries, hard work is praised as the road to "heaven," "the American Dream," or "Utopia." As Russell suggests,

> *For ages, the rich and their sycophants have written in praise of "honest toil," have praised the simple life, have professed a religion which teaches that the poor are much more likely to go to heaven than the rich, and in general have tried to make manual workers believe that there is some special nobility about altering the position of matter in space, just as men tried to make women believe that they derived some special nobility from their sexual enslavement.*[244]

There are voices that demand the reduction of the workday from eight to six, or even four hours, but that won't be enough because the problem is systemic. On the one hand, there is the political element that Rancière describes as the Hatred of Democracy: the system's fear of a broader empowerment of the people, as a result of which the system actively resists every spatial and temporal ground from which an active citizenry can emerge.[245] It is a similar line of thinking that has led George Orwell to the conclusion that when the ruling classes conceive the majority of people as being simply a mob—too dangerous if given too much room—the elites invent ways to keep the people busy even by the means of useless work.[246]

On the other hand, there is the economic element of capitalism, which since the dawn of industrialism, Russell suggests, lays too much stress on production and too little on ordinary living.[247] This obsession with productivity (either of actual goods or services) has developed today into what Graeber calls a "bizarre sadomasochistic dialectic" whereby we feel that pain in the workplace is the only possible justification for our furtive consumer pleasures.[248]

So, although there may be all sorts of technological preconditions for a life based on fewer jobs and more leisure, there are deeply seated political, economic, and psychological reasons that actively resist one such perspective. In its attempts to maintain scarcity, toil, and poverty, the nation-state-capital complex appears increasingly irrational, or as Bookchin puts it, as "the most artificial society in history."[249] Thus, the question of free time is clearly of a political nature.

The order of the day should be then, to develop and advance forms of democratic self-management that place people in charge of the very instituting of society, i.e., a transition to what Castoriadis calls "self-institution."[250] In one such condition all members of society will not only be able to directly participate (without representative intermediates) in how social and individual time is parceled, but also the very content with which it is being filled. In this way one gets beyond merely workers' management of the production, and instead opens paths towards its transformation into a joyful and creative activity, with workplaces effectively embedded into the wider community. If society does not take over the management of the political realm—the sphere that sets the rules and pace of our general life in common—then we run the risk of retaining the current economistic and bureaucratic grip over temporality, and simply pamper it with a more cooperative and humane image.

One such political approach will also change the way people spend their free time. The direct-democratic setting described above has also an educational character that holds the potential of developing anthropological types and attitudes that have passion for law making, critical thinking, and rational exploration. Thus, it creates preconditions to not only change the content of work, but also the one of free time as well, corresponding to Russell's suggestion that we need education that can enable people to use their leisure intelligently.[251] He reaches that conclusion after observing the increasingly passive forms of amusement that tend to occupy the free time of urban populations.[252] In a system in which public affairs are decided upon on at open assemblies by the majority of the population with rational deliberation, and nothing is predetermined by extra-social sources, curiosity and philosophy may well become tangible characteristics of everyday life.

The question of leisure is ultimately a political issue. A reduction of work time in the here and now is a much-welcomed thing, as it will reduce the general feeling of overtiredness and can provide much needed breathing space. But in the long run the goal should be a radical change of the very content of time in and outside of work. As Castoriadis has pointed out, people power is not a backyard of leisure attached to the industrial prison, or providing more gadgets to the prisoners, but the destruction of the industrial prison itself.[253]

Endnotes

Introduction

1 Dimitris Roussopoulos, *Political Ecology: System Change, Not Climate Change* (Montreal: Black Rose Books, 2019), 8.

2 Peter Kalmus, "Forget Plans to Lower Emissions by 2050—This is Deadly Procrastination," *The Guardian*, September 10, 2021, https://bit.ly/3SrtGWl.

3 "COP26: Greta Thunberg Tells Protest that COP26 has been a 'Failure,'" *BBC*, November 5, 2021, https://bbc.in/3SBJwgX.

4 Aubrey Allegretti, "Boris Johnson Says Chances of COP26 Success are 'Touch and Go,'" *The Guardian*, October 25, 2021, https://bit.ly/3Q5LHba.

5 Matt McGrath, "COP26: Fossil Fuel Industry Has Largest Delegation at Climate Summit," *BBC*, November 8, 2021, https://bbc.in/3bwRdVj.

6 Cornelius Castoriadis, "The Problem with Democracy Today," *Athene Antenna*, https://bit.ly/3Q6XTbH.

7 Laura Lynch, host, "Cities Want More of a Say in Fighting Climate Change," What On Earth? (podcast), October 21, 2021, accessed August 7, 2022, https://bit.ly/3zDVpui.

CITIES

Time to Reclaim the City

8 Henri Lefebvre, *The Production of Space* (New Jersey: Blackwell, 1991), 59.

9 Antonio Negri, *Goodbye Mr. Socialism* (New York: Seven Stories Press, 2006), 35.

10 See Franco "Bifo" Berardi, *Heroes: Mass Murder and Suicide* (London: Verso, 2015) and *Dark City*, directed by Alex Proyas (Mystery Clock Cinemas, 1998).

11 See Mike Davis, *Planet of Slums* (London: Verso, 2006).

12 Mark Purcell, "Deleuze and Guattari: Democrats," *Path to the Possible*, July 23, 2013, https://bit.ly/3Q9lrMV.

13 Richard Sennett, *The Fall of Public Man* (New York: Knopf, 1977).

14 Peter G. Goheen, "Public Space and The Geography of the Modern City," *Progress in Human Geography* (August 1998): 482.

15 Max Holleran, "The Neo-Rurals: Spain's 'Lost Generation' Heads for the Hills," *Dissent Magazine*, November 19, 2014, https://bit.ly/3dg7xKx.

16 Lefebvre, *The Production of Space*, 422.

17 David Harvey, *Rebel Cities* (London: Verso, 2012), 4.

18 Charalampos Tsavdaroglou, " The Newcomers' Right to the Common Space: The case of Athens during the refugee crisis," *ACME An International Journal for Critical Geographies*, 17, no. 2, (2018): 376–401.

19 "The Battle for Attica Square – Greece," 2010, https://bit.ly/3QuA9hG.

20 Alex Hibbert, "Homeless Rights Activists Occupy Empty City Centre Office Block and Vow to Help Rough Sleepers," *Manchester Evening News*, Oct 7, 2015, https://bit.ly/3A37DwH.

21 "Guerilla Gardening," *Wikipedia*, https://bit.ly/3pmHjc2.

22 The Liz Christy Garden is a community garden in New York, USA, started on 1973. "Community Gardening," *Wikipedia*, https://bit.ly/2RwCa1S.

23 The Diggers were Protestant radicals in England, often viewed as predecessors of modern anarchism. They were aiming at social change through the creation of small egalitarian rural communities. See Nicolas Walter, "Anarchism and Religion," *The Anarchist Library*, Jan 1, 1999, https://bit.ly/3A1LCOM.

24 Simon Sadler, *The Situationist City* (Michigan: The MIT Press, 1999), 110.

25 During his service in the Florentine Committee, Dante participated in the preparation and planning of San Procolo street widening. See Christopher Alexander, *The Oregon Experiment* (Oxford: Oxford University Press, 1975), 45, 46.

26 See Cornelius Castoriadis, "The Greek Polis and the Creation of Democracy," *Graduate Faculty Philosophy Journal* 9, no. 2 (Fall 1983) and Castoriadis, "Complexity, Magmas, History: The Example of the Medieval Town," 1993.

Exploring Commons-Based Strategies for Urban Regeneration

27 Yavor Tarinski, ed., *Enlightenment and Ecology: The Legacy of Murray Bookchin in the 21st Century* (Montreal: Black Rose Books, 2021), 46.

28 Rudolf Rocker, *Nationalism and Culture* (Chicago: University of Chicago Press, 1937).

Endnotes

29 Alison Pullen and Carl Rhodes, *Bits of Organization* (Copenhagen: Copenhagen Business School Press, 2009), 148.

30 Jonathan Matthew Smucker, "What's Wrong with Activism," *Films for Action*, May 15, 2019, https://bit.ly/3QPA3kY.

31 W. Dennis Keating, "Villages in Cities: Community Land Ownership, Cooperative Housing, and the Milton Parc Story," *Journal of Urban Affairs*, 42, no. 6, (March 2020): 946-948. DOI: 10.1080/07352166.2020.1726668.

The City as Locus for Politics Beyond Statecraft

32 Cornelius Castoriadis, *The Castoriadis Reader* (New Jersey: Blackwell Publishers, 1997), 406-410.

33 Harvey, *Rebel Cities*, 117.

34 Castoriadis, *The Castoriadis Reader*, 267-289.

35 Murray Bookchin, *From Urbanization to Cities* (London: Cassel, 1995), 62-81.

36 Ibid., "The Communalist Project," *New Compass*, February 19, 2011, https://bit.ly/3Rh1FiE.

37 Walter Benjamin, *Selected Writings, Volume 4 1938-40* (Boston: The Belknap Press of Harvard University, 2003), 392.

38 Yessenia Funes, "People in 300+ Cities are Taking Part in the #NoDAPL Day of Action," *Colorlines*, November 15, 2016, https://bit.ly/3AUrPTf.

39 Cornelius Castoriadis, *Figures of the Thinkable* (Redwood City: Stanford University Press, 2005), 146.

Beyond Statecraft Anti-Imperialism

40 Yassin al-Haj Saleh, "The Syrian Cause and Anti-Imperialism," *Yassin al-Haj Saleh*, May 5, 2017, https://bit.ly/3RashBU.

41 Murray Bookchin, "Nationalism and the 'National Question,'" *Libcom*, October 9, 2014, https://bit.ly/3TkXOmu.

42 Gershom Gorenberg, "The Strange Sympathy of the Far Left for Putin," *The American Prospect*, October 14, 2016, https://bit.ly/3cucGyA.

43 Cornelius Castoriadis, *A Society Adrift* (New York: Fordham University Press, 2010), 243.

44 Stuart Jeanne Bramhall, "The Arab Spring: Made in the USA," *Global Research*, October 25, 2015, https://bit.ly/3Ksmjdv.

45 Dan Radnika, "Rojava: The Fraud of a Non-existent Social Revolution," *Libcom*, June 27, 2017, https://bit.ly/3ToGH3t.

123

46 Saleh, "The Syrian Cause and Anti-Imperialism."

47 Rohini Hensman, *Indefensible* (Chicago: Haymarket Books, 2018).

48 Meredith Tax, "Supporting Dictators is not Anti-Imperialism," *Roar*, June 26, 2019, https://bit.ly/3wwec9V.

49 Murray Bookchin, "Nationalism."

50 Ibid.

51 Ibid.

52 Rahman Bouzari, "Iranian Pseudo Anti-Imperialism," *Open Democracy*, October 18, 2018, https://bit.ly/3QUKoMz.

Municipalist Commoning and Factory Recuperation

53 Marina Sitrin, "Recuperating Work and Life," *Roar*, https://bit.ly/3CSIWpZ.

Emancipated Neighborhoods within the Project of Direct Democracy

54 Jane Jacobs, *The Death and Life of Great American Cities* (New York: Vintage Books, 1961), 238.

55 Ira Harkavy & Lee Benson, "De-Platonizing and Democratizing Education as the Bases of Service Learning," *Service Learning* 73 (Spring 1998): 17.

56 John Dewey, "The School as a Social Center," *The Elementary School Teacher* 3, no.2 (October 1902): 84.

57 Cornelius Castoriadis, *Postscript on Insignificancy* (London: Bloomsbury, 2017), 147.

58 Murray Bookchin, "Libertarian Municipalism: An Overview," *Green Perspectives*, no.24 (October 1991).

59 Stavros Stavrides, *Common Space: The City as Commons* (London: Zed Books, 2016), 56.

60 Dimitri Roussopoulos, "The Democratic Project of Milton Parc," *Trise*, https://bit.ly/3Awd07E.

61 Julius Gavroche, "Acapatzingo: An Autonomous Community in Resistance," *Autonomies*, September 7, 2021, https://bit.ly/3ASYl8g [21] & Evan Neuhausen, "A Project for Life in Mexico City," *NACLA*, January 6, 2020, https://bit.ly/3KoqdnL.

62 Op. Cit. 61

63 "Community of Squatted Prosfygika," *Trise*, December 20, 2021, https://bit.ly/3KvdiRa.

Against Police Brutality: Towards Cities of Self-Limitation

64 Network for an Alternative Quest, *Challenging Capitalist Modernity II: Dissecting Capitalist Modernity: Building Democratic Confederalism* (Neuss: International Initiative, 2015), 301-302.

65 Yavor Tarinski, "Self-Limitation and Democracy," *Public Seminar*, February 7, 2018, https://bit.ly/3Aree4h.

66 Elizabeth Baughman, "Scythian Archers," *Demos*, January 30, 2003, https://bit.ly/3AsE3Rq.

67 Yannis Andricopoulos, *The Cultural Challenge: A Trilogy* (Exeter: Imprint Academic, 2017).

68 Stella Tsolakidou, "The Police in Ancient Greece," *Greek Reporter*, May 30, 2013, https://bit.ly/3AU06SD.

69 "Commune," *Britannica*, August 20, 2022, https://bit.ly/3R4FZGL.

70 David Whitehouse, "Origins of the Police," *Libcom*, https://bit.ly/3ctjyw9.

71 Paul Foot, "The Last Time Paris Went Left," *The Guardian*, March 20, 2001, https://bit.ly/3wLtCr5.

72 Jeffrey Monaghan, "Surveillance and Society," *Queens University Library*, 2012, https://bit.ly/3wJdjLk.

73 Davide Panagi, *The Political Life of Sensation* (Durham: Duke University Press, 2009), 121.

74 Whitehouse, "Origins of the Police."

Federations of Cities: Castoriadis, Bookchin, AANES

75 Castoriadis, *Figures of the Thinkable*, 352.

76 Ibid., *A Society Adrift*.

77 Jonathan Bennett, "Jean-Jacques Rousseau: The Social Contract," 2017, 34, https://bit.ly/2wa6oL3.

78 Castoriadis, *Postscript on Insignificancy*, 105.

79 Ibid., *The Castoriadis Reader*, 311.

80 Ibid., *Postscript on Insignificancy*, 105.

81 Ibid., *The Castoriadis Reader*, 58.

82 Castoriadis, *The Castoriadis Reader*, 89.

83 Ibid., "The Problem with Democracy."

84 Ibid., *The Castoriadis Reader*, 95.

85 Castoriadis , *The Castoriadis Reader*, 95.

86 Ibid., *Postscript on Insignificancy*, 152.

87 Ibid., *Democracy and Relativism* (Lanham: Rowman & Littlefield, 2013), 42.
88 Castoriadis, *Democracy and Relativism*, 43.
89 Ibid., *Postscript on Insignificancy*,152.
90 Ibid., 152.
91 Ibid., *A Society Adrift*, 134.
92 Ibid., 134.
93 Ibid., 146-147.
94 Ibid.
95 David Graeber, *Utopia of Rules* (New York: Melville House, 2015), 31.
96 Castoriadis, *A Society Adrift*, 146-147.
97 Pierre-Joseph, Proudhon, "The Federative Principle," *The Anarchist Library*, https://bit.ly/3BedOQs.
98 Bookchin, "Libertarian Municipalism."
99 Bookchin, "Libertarian Municipalism."
100 *Castoriadis, The Castoriadis Reader*, 251.
101 Cornelius Castoriadis, "The Greek Polis and the Creation of Democracy," *Graduate Faculty Philosophy Journal* 9, no. 2 (Fall 1983)
102 Castoriadis, *A Society Adrift*, 191.
103 Ibid., 191.
104 Zanyar Omrani, "Introduction to the Political and Social Structures of Democratic Autonomy in Rojava," *Cooperation in Mesopotamia*, https://bit.ly/3qbHrve.
105 Ibid.
106 Omrani, "Political and Social Structures."
107 Jack Jershaw, "What Can We Learn from Rojava," *UCLPI Media*, https://bit.ly/3cMJin6.
108 The communities that constitute the movement of the Zapatistas have built a de facto autonomous system of self-governance in the Mexican state of Chiapas.
109 Castoriadis, *Postscript on Insignificancy*, 152.

The Temporalities of Climate Change: From Domination to Direct Democracy

110 Castoriadis, *The Castoriadis Reader*, 247.
111 Anatol Lieven, *Climate Change and the Nation State* (Oxford: Oxford University Press, 2020).

112 François-Marie Bréon, "La lute pour le climat est contraire aux libertés individuelles," *Liberation*, July 29, 2018, https://bit.ly/3cPawJV.

113 Paolo Virno, *Deja Vu and The End of History* (London: Verso Books, 2015), 18.

114 Murray Bookchin, *Post-Scarcity Anarchism* (Montreal: Black Rose Books, 1986), 71.

115 Castoriadis, *A Society Adrift*, 248.

116 "What Is Social Ecology," *Institute for Social Ecology*, https://bit.ly/3q95ivC.

117 Kristin Ross, *A Coffee with Kristin Ross: On the Continuations of May '68* (Athens: Babylonia, 2019), 5-6.

118 James D. Cockcroft, "Review of Shadows of Tender Fury," *Science and Society* 62, no. 2 (Summer 1998), https://bit.ly/3AVbL2q.

119 Ana Dinerstein, "The Speed of the Snail: The Zapatistas' Autonomy de facto and the Mexican State," *Econstor*, https://bit.ly/3TMc08C.

120 Erich Mühsam, *The Creation of the Bavarian Council Republic: From Eisner to Levine* (Athens: Vivliopelagos, 2020), 39.

121 Richard Greeman, "Yellow Vests Struggle to Reinvent Democracy," *SP The Bullet*, April 17, 2019. https://bit.ly/3wXKJ98.

122 John Dryzek, "Deliberative Democracy and Climate Change," *Humans Nature*, January 14, 2013, https://bit.ly/3q7s6fn.

123 Castoriadis, *A Society Adrift*, 249

124 Op. Cit. 123

CITIZENS

Citizenship as an Inseparable Part of Revolutionary Politics

125 Derek Heater, *A Brief History of Citizenship* (New York City: New York University Press, 2004), 157

126 Lynette Shultz, "Educating for Global Citizenship: Conflicting Agendas and Understandings," *The Alberta Journal of Educational Research* 53, no. 3 (2007): 249

127 Aristotle, *The Politics* (Chicago: The University of Chicago Press, 1984), 87.

128 Ibid., 37.

129 Ibid., 87.

130 Castoriadis, *The Castoriadis Reader*, 56.

131 Ibid., 280.

132 Ibid., 281.

133 Castoriadis, *The Castoriadis Reader*, 288.

134 Ibid., 288.

135 John Merrick, "Citoyennes et citoyens," *Verso*, July 14, 2015, https://bit.ly/3enkpz4.

136 Elie Reclus, *La Commune de Paris, au jour le jour, 1871, 19 Mars–28 Mai* (Paris: Schleicher frères, 1908), 46.

137 Merrick, "Citoyennes et citoyens."

138 Andrew Light, "Ecological Citizenship: The Democ ratic Promise of Restoration," in *The Humane Metropolis: People and Nature in the 21st Century City*, ed. R. Platt (Amherst: University of Massachusetts Press, 2005).

139 S.T.A. Pickett, Mary Cadenasso, Morgan Grove, & Charles Nilon, "Urban Ecological Systems: Linking Terrestrial Ecological, Physical, and Socioeconomic Components of Metropolitan Areas," *Annual Review of Ecology and Systematics*, no. 32 (November 2003).

140 Murray Bookchin, "What Is Social Ecology," *Anarchy Archives*, https://bit.ly/3Bf8pbB.

141 Castoriadis, "The Problem of Democracy Today."

142 Thomas Jefferson, *Michael Hardt Presents the Declaration of Independence* (London: Verso, 2007), 62-63.

Citizens or Workers

143 Thomas Paine, *Rights of Man* (Ware: Wordsworth Classics of World Literature, 1996), 171.

144 Geneviève Azam, "Hannah Arendt and Karl Polanyi: Economic Liberalism, the Political Collpase, and Mass Society," *Revue du MAUSS* 34, no. 2 (2009), https://bit.ly/3RjcG3x.

145 Franz Borkenau, *World Communism* (Michigan: University of Michigan Press, 1962), 57-79.

146 Murray Bookchin, "The Ghost of Anarcho-Syndicalism," *Libcom*, March 18, 2014, https://bit.ly/3qc6K0b.

147 Cornelius Castoriadis, "Imagining Society," *Variant* 1 (1993): 42.

148 "Hannah Arendt," *Stanford Encyclopedia of Philosophy*, 2019, https://stanford.io/2vt50mK.

149 Lawrence Liang, "Interview with Jacques Rancière," *Kafila*, December 2, 2009, https://bit.ly/3cMoFYi.

150 Bookchin, "The Ghost of Anarcho-Syndicalism."

151 Castoriadis, *The Castoriadis Reader*, 8.

152 Murray Bookchin, *The Next Revolution: Popular Assemblies & The Promise of Direct Democracy* (London: Verso, 2015), 29.

153 Richard Sandbrook, "Why Polanyi and Not Marx?" *Progressive Futures Blog*, May 2, 2015, https://bit.ly/3cMzhXk.

The Spatial Dimensions of Citizenship versus Mob Rule

154 Hannah Arendt, *The Origins of Totalitarianism* (London: Harcourt, 1973), 307.

155 Timothy Snowball, "The United States is Not a Democracy, and It Wasn't Meant to Be One," *The Hill*, October 29, 2018, https://bit.ly/3RB2GlU.

156 Arendt, *The Origins of Totalitarianism*, 107.

157 Ibid., 238.

158 Hannah Arendt, *The Human Condition* (London: The University of Chicago Press, 1998), 203.

159 Hannah Arendt, *The Origins of Totalitarianism*, 107.

160 Ibid., 382.

161 Ibid., 249.

162 Ibid., 337.

163 Arendt, *The Origins of Totalitarianism*, 107.

164 Jean-Yves Camus & Nicolas Lebourg, *Far-Right Politics in Europe* (Cambridge: The Belknap Press, 2017), 12.

165 Hannah Arendt, *On Revolution* (New York: Penguin Books, 2006), 230.

166 Bennett, "Jean-Jacques Rousseau: The Social Contract."

167 Castoriadis, "The Problem of Democracy Today."

168 "Hannah Arendt," *Stanford Encyclopedia of Philosophy*.

169 Hannah Arendt, *On Revolution*, 245.

170 Ibid., 271.

171 Arendt, *On Revolution*, 255-256.

172 Ibid., 245.

From Pseudo-Rationalism to Rationality as Quality of Thought

173 Janet Biehl (ed.), *The Murray Bookchin Reader* (Montreal: Black Rose Books, 1999), 39.

174 Hannah Arendt, *Between Past and Future: Eight Exercises in Political Thought* (New York: The Viking Press, 1961), 5.

175 Charles Taylor, Patrizia Nanz, & Madeleine Beaubien Taylor, *Reconstructing Democracy: How Citizens are Building from the Ground Up* (Cambridge: Harvard University Press, 2020), 60-61.

176 Castoriadis, *The Castoriadis Reader*, 240.

177 Slavoj Zizek, "Slavoj Zizek on Direct Democracy," November 23, 2016, https://bit.ly/3x58wEt.

178 "Ancient Greek Democracy," *History*, September 16, 2021, https://bit.ly/2J1Csah. & Andranik, Tangian, *Theory of Democracy* (Berlin: Springer Berlin Heidelberg, 2013).

179 Castoriadis, *The Castoriadis Reader* (Oxford: Blackwell Publishers, 1997), 393.

180 Ingerid S. Straume and Giorgio Baruchello eds., *Creation, Rationality and Autonomy: Essays on Cornelius Castoriadis* (Aarhus: Aarhus University Press, 2013), 19.

181 Ibid., 20.

182 Janet Biehl ed., *The Murray Bookchin Reader*, 39.

183 Ibid., 98.

184 Castoriadis, *The Castoriadis Reader*, 390.

185 Ibid., 391.

186 Biehl ed., *The Murray Bookchin Reader*, 66.

187 Murray Bookchin, "Free Cities: Communalism and the Left," *Libcom*, February 6, 2020, https://bit.ly/3BmDMjF.

188 "A 'Long and Patient Work of Preparation,' In an Age of Catastrophe: Remarks on Castoriadis' Political Legacy," *Aftoleksi*, June 18, 2022, https://bit.ly/3KYgjcN.

Overcoming Individualist Passivity: Freedom as Political Action

189 Isaiah Berlin, *The Roots of Romanticism* (Oxford: Princeton University Press, 2013), 64.

190 Marshall Sinclair, "Why the Self-Help Industry is Dominating the US," *Medium*, February 24, 2019, https://bit.ly/3AUXhiI.

191 Berlin, *The Roots of Romanticism*, 44.

192 Ibid.

193 Hannah Arendt, *The Freedom to be Free* (New York: Penguin Books, 2020), 51-52.

194 Arendt, *The Freedom to be Free*, 45.

195 Ibid., 59.

196 Castoriadis, *The Castoriadis Reader*, 150.

197 Arendt, *The Freedom to be Free*, 72.

198 Ibid., 34.

199 Ibid., 74.

200 Castoriadis, *The Castoriadis Reader*, 275.

201 Ibid., 276.

Identities, Space, Time, and Emancipation

202 Kristin Ross, *Communal Luxury: The Political Imaginary of the Paris Commune* (New York: Verso 2015), 14.

203 Cole Strangler, "What's Really Behind France's Yellow Vest Protest?" *The Nation*, December 7, 2018, https://bit.ly/3U7DJRg.

204 "'Yellow Vests' Open a New Front in The Battle: Popular Referendums," *France 24*, December 17, 2018, https://bit.ly/2EJOLsq.

205 Kristin Ross, *The Emergence of Social Space: Rimbaud and the Paris Commune* (New York: Verso 2008), 22.

206 Prosper-Olivier Lissagaray, "18th March 1871: Prosper-Olivier Lissagaray on The Establishment of the Paris Commune," *Verso*, March 18, 2016, https://bit.ly/3RuaN40.

207 Yavor Tarinski, "Interview with Kristin Ross," *Babylonia*, May 25, 2018, https://bit.ly/3L7YTdY.

208 Ross, *The Emergence of Social Space*, 5.

209 Ibid., 17-18.

210 Ibid., 13-14.

211 Kristin Ross, *The Emergence of Social Space*, 13.

212 Jacques Rancière, *Nights of Labor: The Workers' Dream in Nineteenth-Century France* (Philadelphia: Temple University Press, 1989), xxix.

213 Kristin Ross, "Nothing and Everything: The Zad Victory," *Verso*, January 22, 2018, https://bit.ly/3BqDLez.

214 Victoria Brunetta & Kate O'Shea, eds., *Durty Words: A Space for Dialogue, Solidarity, Resistance and Creation* (Limerick: Durty Books, 2018), 275.

215 Patrick Isensee, "What Is the Right to The City?" *Rio On Watch*, October 16, 2013, https://bit.ly/3QE3HbP.

216 Sveinung Legard, "Popular Assemblies in Revolts and Revolutions," *New Compass*, August 7, 2011, https://bit.ly/3d23vpo.

217 Roger Gregoire & Fredy Perlman, "Worker-Student Action Committees: France May '68," *The Anarchist Library*, January 18, 2010, https://bit.ly/3d7xYCn.

218 Strangler, "What's Really Behind France's Yellow Vest Protest?"

219 Kristin Ross, "The Long 1960s and 'The Wind from The West,'" *Crisis & Critique* 5, no. 2 (November 2018): 325.

220 Ross, *The Emergence of Social Space*, 7.

221 Kristin Ross, *May '68 and its Afterlives* (Chicago: University of Chicago Press, 2002), 65.

222 Jacques Rancière, "Jacques Rancière on the Gilets Jaunes Protests," *Verso*, February 12, 2019, https://bit.ly/2X45ht9.

223 Ibid.

Sortition and the Public Assembly

224 Aristotle, "Politics", Book 5, Section 1301a, https://bit.ly/3Sf0IZk.

225 "List of Direct Democracy Parties," *Wikipedia*, August 19, 2022, https://bit.ly/3xalwZi.

226 Aristotle, "Politics", Book 4, Section 1294b, https://bit.ly/3DVSn-FD.

227 Aristotle, "Politics", Book 3, Section 1277b, https://bit.ly/3r5bpBy.

228 Dacher Keltner, "The Power Paradox," *Greater Good Magazine*, December 1, 2007, https://bit.ly/3eGg2PG.

229 "Foucault: Power is Everywhere," *Powercube*, https://bit.ly/2Gf5uoU.

230 Erik Olin Wright, *Envisioning Real Utopias* (London: Verso, 2010), 171.

231 Boule (Greek: βουλή, "council, assembly"): a council of citizens appointed to run the daily affairs of the city. After the reforms made by Cleisthenes the size of the boule was expanded to 500 men chosen by lot from all citizens. "Boule (Ancient Greece)," *Wikipedia*, July 2022, https://bit.ly/3TWUtdM.

232 Amy Lang, "But Is it For Real? The British Columbia Citizen's Assembly as a Model of State-Sponsored Citizen Empowerment," *Politics & Society* (March 2007).

233 Single Transferable Vote (STV) is organized around multimember districts, which increases the proportional distribution of seats, if the districts have enough members. STV also uses a preferential ballot to rank other candidates in each district. In practice, candidates from the same party compete against one another for vote's preferences, as in a primary system, giving voters more choice about who will be their representative, and

undermining a party's ability to control the candidate from that district. "BC STV," *Wikipedia*, November 2021, https://bit.ly/3RDfjgI.

Educational Approaches towards Democratic Citizenry

234 Yaacov Hecht, "The Future of Education: Georges Haddad and Yaacov Hecht at World Forum for Democracy 2016," *Open Democracy*, December 12, 2016, https://bit.ly/3TY9yvz.

235 Cornelius Castoriadis, "The Crisis of Modern Society," *Libcom*, September 19, 2013, https://bit.ly/3U3cEi7.

236 Bernhard Schmidt Hertha, Sabina Jelenc Krašovec, Marvin Formosa eds., *Learning across Generations in Europe: Contemporary Issues in Older Adult Education* (Rotterdam: Sense Publishers, 2014), 28.

237 Ivan Illich, *Deschooling Society* (Harmondsworth: Marion Boyars Publishers Ltd, 1973), 78.

238 Paulo Freire, *Teachers as Cultural Workers: Letters to Those Who Dare Teach* (Boulder: Westview Press, 1998), 31.

239 Yaacov Hecht, "Notes from the Opening Plenary: Towards Teachers and Students Deciding on 20% of the Curriculum Together," *Open Democracy*, November 15, 2016, https://bit.ly/3RWCEKc.

240 Richard Bailey, *A.S. Neill* (London: Bloomsbury, 2013), 131.

Time, Leisure, Work:
Towards a Radical Transformation of Everyday Life

241 David Graeber, *Bullshit Jobs: A Theory* (London: Penguin Books, 2018), XXIV.

242 Bertrand Russell, *In Praise of Idleness* (New York: Routledge, 2004), 5-6.

243 Russell, *In Praise of Idleness*, 5.

244 Russell, *In Praise of Idleness*, 9.

245 Jacques Rancière, *Hatred of Democracy* (London: Verso, 2014).

246 George Orwell, *Down and Out in Paris and London* (Oxford: Oxford University Press, 2021), 94.

247 Russell, *In Praise of Idleness*, 36.

248 Graeber, *Bullshit Jobs: A Theory*, 246.

249 Bookchin, *Post-Scarcity Anarchism*, 17.

250 Yavor Tarinski, "Self-Limitation and Democracy," *Public Seminar,* February 7, 2018, https://bit.ly/3qtPsMp.
251 Russell, *In Praise of Idleness,* 12.
252 Ibid., 22.
253 Castoriadis, *The Castoriadis Reader,* 131.

Bibliography

"A Long and Patient Work of Preparation,' In an Age of Catastrophe: Remarks on Castoriadis' Political Legacy," *Aftoleksi*, June 18, 2022, https://bit.ly/3KYgjcN.

Alexander, Christopher. *The Oregon Experiment*. Oxford: Oxford University Press, 1975.

Allegretti, Aubrey. "Boris Johnson Says Chances of COP26 Success are 'Touch and Go.'" *The Guardian*. October 25, 2021. https://bit.ly/3Q5LHba.

"Ancient Greek Philosophy." *History*. September 16, 2021, https://bit.ly/2J1Csah.

Andricopoulos, Yannis. *The Cultural Challenge: A Trilogy*. Exeter: Imprint Academic, 2017.

Arendt, Hannah. *Between Past and Future: Eight Exercises in Political Thought*. New York: The Viking Press, 1961.

_____. *On Revolution*. London: Penguin Books, 2006.

_____. *The Freedom to be Free*. New York: Penguin Books, 2020.

_____. *The Human Condition*. London: The University of Chicago Press, 1998.

_____. *The Origins of Totalitarianism*. San Diego: A Harvest Book, 1979.

Aristotle, *The Politics*. Chicago: The University of Chicago Press, 1984.

Azam, Genevieve. "Hannah Arendt and Karl Polanyi: Economic Liberalism, the Political Collapse, and Mass Society." *Revue du MAUSS* 34, no. 2 (2009). https://bit.ly/3RjcG3x.

Bailey, Richard. *A.S. Neill*. London: Bloomsbury, 2013.

Baughman, Elizabeth. "Scythian Archers." *Demos*. January 30, 2003. https://bit.ly/3AsE3Rq.

"BC STV." *Wikipedia*. November 2021. https://bit.ly/3RDfjgI.

Bennett, Jonathan. "Jean-Jacques Rousseau: The Social Contract." 2017. https://bit.ly/2wa6oL3.

Benjamin, Walter. *Selected Writings, Volume 4 1938-40*. Boston: The Belknap Press of Harvard University, 2003.

Berlin, Isaiah. *The Roots of Romanticism*. Oxford: Princeton University Press, 2013.

Biehl, Janet. *The Murray Bookchin Reader*. Montreal: Black Rose Books, 1999.

_____. *The Politics of Social Ecology: Libertarian Municipalism*. Montreal: Black Rose Books, 1997.

Bollier, David & Silke Helfrich, eds. *The Wealth of the Commons: A World Beyond Market and State*. Amherst: Levellers Press, 2015.

Bookchin, Murray. "Free Cities: Communalism and the Left," *Libcom*. February 6, 2020. https://bit.ly/3BmDMjF.

_____. *From Urbanization to Cities*. London: Cassel, 1995.

_____. "Libertarian Municipalism: An Overview." *Green Perspectives*, no. 24 (October 1991).

_____. "Nationalism and the 'National Question.'" *Libcom*. October 9, 2014. https://bit.ly/3TkXOmu.

_____. *Deja Vu and The End of History*. London: Verso Books, 2015.

_____. "The Communalist Project." *New Compass*. February 19, 2011. https://bit.ly/3Rh1FiE.

_____. "The Ghost of Anarcho-Syndicalism." *Libcom*. March 18, 2014. https://bit.ly/3qc6K0b.

_____. *The Next Revolution: Popular Assemblies and the Promise of Direct Democracy*. New York: Verso, 2015.

_____. *The Philosophy of Social Ecology: Essays on Dialectical Naturalism*, Montreal: Black Rose Books, 1996.

_____. *Urbanization Without Cities: The Rise and Decline of Citizenship*. Montreal: Black Rose Books, 1996.

_____. "What Is Social Ecology," *Anarchy Archives*, https://bit.ly/3Bf8pbB.

Borkenau, Franz. *World Communism*. Michigan: University of Michigan Press, 1962.

"Boule (Ancient Greece)." *Wikipedia*. July 2022. https://bit.ly/3TWUtdM.

Bouzari, Rahman. "Iranian Pseudo Anti-Imperialism." *Open Democracy*. October 18, 2018. https://bit.ly/3QUKoMz.

Bramhall, Stuart Jeanne. "The Arab Spring: Made in the USA." *Global Research*. October 25, 2015. https://bit.ly/3Ksmjdv.

Bréon, François-Marie. "La lute pour le climat est contraire aux libertés individuelles." *Liberation*. July 29, 2018. https://bit.ly/3cPawJV.

Brunetta, Victoria & Kate O'Shea, eds. *Durty Words: A Space for Dialogue, Solidarity, Resistance and Creation*. Limerick: Durty Books, 2018.

Cabannes, Yves. *Another City is Possible with Participatory Budgeting*. Montreal: Black Rose Books, 2017.

Camus, Jean-Yves & Nicolas Lebourg. *Far-Right Politics in Europe*. Cambridge: The Belknap Press, 2017.

Castoriadis, Cornelius. *A Society Adrift*. New York: Fordham University Press, 2010.

_____. "Complexity, Magmas, History: The Example of the Medieval Town." 1993.

_____. *Democracy and Relativism*. Lanham: Rowman & Littlefield, 2013.

_____. *Figures of the Thinkable*. Redwood City: Stanford University Press, 2005

_____. "Imagining Society." *Variant* 1 (1993): 42.

_____. *Postscript on Insignificancy*. London: Bloomsbury, 2017.

_____. *Political and Social Writings Volume 1*. Minneapolis: University of Minnesota Press, 1988.

_____. *Political and Social Writings Volume 2*. Minneapolis: University of Minnesota Press, 1988.

_____. *Political and Social Writings Volume 3*. Minneapolis: University of Minnesota Press, 1993.

_____. "The Crisis of Modern Society." *Libcom* September 19, 2013. https://bit.ly/3U3cFi7.

_____. "The Greek Polis and the Creation of Democracy." *Graduate Faculty Philosophy Journal* 9, no. 2 (Fall 1983).

_____. *The Imaginary Institution of Society*. Cambridge: MIT Press, 1998.

_____. "The Problem with Democracy Today." *Athene Antenna*. https://bit.ly/3Q6XTbH.

_____. *The Rising Tide of Insignificancy: The Big Sleep*. New York: Not Bored! 2003.

_____. *Workers' Councils and the Economics of a Self-Managed Society*. Johannesburg: Zabalaza Books, 2007.

_____. *The Castoriadis Reader*. Oxford: Blackwell Publishers, 1997.

Cockcroft, James D. "Review of Shadows of Tender Fury." *Science and Society* 62, no. 2 (Summer 1998). https://bit.ly/3AVbL2q.

"Commune." *Britannica*. August 20, 2022. https://bit.ly/3R4FZGL.

"Community Gardening." *Wikipedia*. https://bit.ly/2RwCa1S.

"Community of Squatted Prosfygika." *Trise*. December 20, 2021. https://bit.ly/3KvdiRa.

"COP26: Greta Thunberg Tells Protest that COP26 has been a 'Failure.'" *BBC*. November 5, 2021. https://bbc.in/3SBJwgX.

Dacher, Keltner. "The Power Paradox." *Greater Good Magazine*. December 1, 2007. https://bit.ly/3eGg2PG.

Davis, Mike. *Planet of Slums*. London: Verso, 2007.

Dewey, John. "The School as a Social Center." *The Elementary School Teacher* 3, no. 2 (October 1902): 84.

Dinerstein, Ana. "The Speed of the Snail: The Zapatistas' Autonomy de facto and The Mexican State." *Econstor*. https://bit.ly/3TMc08C.

Dryzek, John. "Deliberative Democracy and Climate Change." *Humans Nature*. January 14, 2013. https://bit.ly/3q7s6fn.

Fleming, Marie. *The Geography of Freedom: The Odyssey of Élisee Reclus*. Montreal: Black Rose Books, 1987.

Foot, Paul. "The Last Time Paris Went Left." *The Guardian*. March 20, 2001. https://bit.ly/3wLtCr5.

"Foucault: Power is Everywhere." *Powercube*. https://bit.ly/2Gf5uoU.

Freire, Paulo. *Teachers as Cultural Workers: Letters to Those Who Dare Teach*. Boulder: Westview Press, 1998.

Funes, Yessenia. "People in 300+ Cities are Taking Part in the #NoDAPL Day of Action." *Colorlines*. November 15, 2016. https://bit.ly/3AUrPTf.

Gavroche, Julius. "Acapatzingo: An Autonomous Community in Resistance." *Autonomies*. September 7, 2021. https://bit.ly/3ASYl8g.

Garcia-Chueca, Eva & Lorenzo Vidal, eds. *Advancing Urban Rights: Equality and Diversity in the City*. Montreal: Black Rose Books, 2022.

Goheen, Peter G. "Public Space and The Geography of the Modern City." *Progress in Human Geography* (August 1998): 482.

Graeber, David. *Bullshit Jobs: A Theory*. London: Penguin Books, 2018.

_____. *Utopia of Rules*. New York: Melville House, 2015.

Graham, Stephen. *Cities Under Siege: The New Military Urbanism*. London: Verso, 2011.

Greeman, Richard. "Yellow Vests Struggle to Reinvent Democracy." *SP The Bullet*. April 17, 2019. https://bit.ly/3wXKJ98.

Gregoire, Roger. "Worker-Student Action Committees: France May '68." *The Anarchist Library*. January 18, 2010. https://bit.ly/3d7xYCn.

Groenberg, Gershom. "The Strange Sympathy of the Far Left for Putin." *The American Prospect*. October 14, 2016. https://bit.ly/3cucGyA.

"Guerilla Gardening." *Wikipedia*. https://bit.ly/3pmHjc2.

Harkavy, Ira and Lee Benson, "De-Platonizing and Democratizing Education as the Bases of Service Learning." *Service Learning* 73 (Spring 1998): 17.

"Hannah Arendt." *Stanford Encyclopedia of Philosophy*. 2019. https://stanford.io/2vt50mK.

Harvey, David. *Rebel Cities: From the Right to the City to the Urban Revolution*. London: Verso, 2012.

Hawley, Joshua & Dimitri Roussopoulos (eds.): *Villages in Cities: Community Land Ownership, Cooperative Housing, and the Milton Parc Story*. Montreal: Black Rose Books, 2019.

Heater, Derek. *A Brief History of Citizenship*. New York City: New York University Press, 2004.

Hecht, Yaacov. "Notes from the Opening Plenary: Towards Teachers and Students Deciding on 20% of the Curriculum Together," *Open Democracy*, November 15, 2016, https://bit.ly/3RWCEKc.

_____. "The Future of Education: Georges Haddad and Yaacov Hecht at World Forum for Democracy 2016." *Open Democracy*. December 12, 2016. https://bit.ly/3TY9yvz.

Hensman, Rohini. *Indefensible*. Chicago: Haymarket Books, 2018.

Hibbert, Alex. "Homeless Rights Activists Occupy Empty City Centre Office Block and Vow to Help Rough Sleepers." *Manchester Evening News*. Oct 7, 2015. https://bit.ly/3A37DwH.

Holleran, Max. "The Neo-Rurals: Spain's 'Lost Generation' Heads for the Hills." *Dissent Magazine*. November 19, 2014, https://bit.ly/3dg7xKx.

Illich, Ivan. *Deschooling Society*. Harmondsworth: Marion Boyars Publishers Ltd, 1973.

Isensee, Patrick. "What Is the Right to The City?" *Rio On Watch*. October 16, 2013. https://bit.ly/3QE3HbP.

Jacobs, Jane. *The Death and Life of Great American Cities*. New York: Vintage Books, 1992.

Jefferson, Thomas. *Michael Hardt Presents the Declaration of Independence*. London: Verso, 2007.

Jershaw, Jack. "What Can We Learn from Rojava." *UCLPI Media*. https://bit.ly/3cMJin6.

Kalmus, Peter. "Forget Plans to Lower Emissions by 2050—This is Deadly Procrastination." *The Guardian*. September 10, 2021. https://bit.ly/3SrtGWl.

Keating, W. Dennis. "Villages in Cities: Community Land Ownership, Cooperative Housing, and the Milton Parc Story." *Journal of Urban Affairs* 42, no. 6 (March 2020): 946-948. DOI: 10.1080/07352166.2020.1726668.

Knapp, Michael et. al. *Revolution in Rojava: Democratic Autonomy and Women's Liberation in the Syrian Kurdistan*. London: Pluto Press, 2016.

Lang, Amy. "But Is it For Real? The British Columbia Citizen's Assembly as a Model of State-Sponsored Citizen Empowerment." *Politics & Society* (March 2007).

Lefebvre, Henri. *Rhythmanalysis: Space, Time and Everyday Life*. London: Bloomsbury, 2013.

_____. *The Production of Space*. Oxford: Blackwell, 1991.

Legard, Sveinung. "Popular Assemblies in Revolts and Revolutions." *New Compass*. August 7, 2011. https://bit.ly/3d23vpo.

Liang, Lawrence. "Interview with Jacques Rancière." *Kafila*. December 2, 2009. https://bit.ly/3cMoFYi.

Lieven, Anatol. *Climate Change and the Nation State*. Oxford: Oxford University Press, 2020.

Lissagaray, Prosper-Olivier. "18th March 1871: Prosper-Olivier Lissagaray on The Establishment of the Paris Commune." *Verso*. March 18, 2016. https://bit.ly/3RuaN40.

"List of Direct Democracy Parties." *Wikipedia*. August 19, 2022. https://bit.ly/3xalwZi.

Lynch, Laura, host. "Cities Want More of a Say in Fighting Climate Change." What On Earth? (podcast). October 21, 2021. Accessed August 7, 2022. https://bit.ly/3zDVpui.

McGrath, Matt. "COP26: Fossil Fuel Industry Has Largest Delegation at Climate Summit." *BBC*. November 8, 2021. https://bbc.in/3bwRdVj.

Merrick, John. "Citoyennes et citoyens." *Verso*. July 14, 2015, https://bit.ly/3enkpz4.

Montgomery, Charles. *Happy City*. Penguin Books, 2015.

Monaghan, Jeffrey. "Surveillance and Society." *Queens University Library*. 2012. https://bit.ly/3wJdjLk.

Mühsam, Erich. *The Creation of the Bavarian Council Republic: From Eisner to Levine.* Athens: Vivliopelagos, 2020.

Negri, Antonio. *Goodbye Mr. Socialism.* New York: Seven Stories Press, 2006.

Negri, Antonio and Michael Hardt. *Commonwealth.* Boston: Belknap Press, 2011.

Network for an Alternative Quest: *Challenging Capitalist Modernity II: Dissecting Capitalist Modernity: Building Democratic Confederalism*. Neuss: International Initiative, 2015.

Neuhausen, Evan. "A Project for Life in Mexico City." *NACLA.* January 6, 2020. https://bit.ly/3KoqdnL.

Omrani, Zanyar. "Introduction to the Political and Social Structures of Democratic Autonomy in Rojava." *Cooperation in Mesopotamia.* https://bit.ly/3qbHrve.

Orwell, George. *Down and Out in Paris and London.* Oxford: Oxford University Press, 2021.

Ostrom, Elinor. *Governing the Commons: The Evolution of Institutions for Collective Action.* Cambridge: Cambridge University Press, 2015.

Panagi, Davide. *The Political Life of Sensation.* Durham: Duke University Press, 2009.

Paine, Thomas. *Rights of Man.* Ware: Wordsworth Classics of World Literature, 1996.

Pickett, STA, Mary Cadenasso, Morgan Grove, & Charles Nilon. "Urban Ecological Systems: Linking Terrestrial Ecological, Physical, and Socioeconomic Components of Metropolitan Areas." *Annual Review of Ecology and Systematics*, no. 32 (November 2003).

Platt, Rutherford, ed. *The Humane Metropolis: People and Nature in the 21st Century City.* Amherst: University of Massachusetts Press, 2005.

Pullen, Alison. *Bits of Organization.* Copenhagen: Copenhagen Business School Press, 2009.

Purcell, Mark. "Deleuze and Guattari: Democrats." *Path to the Possible.* July 23, 2013. https://bit.ly/3Q9lrMV.

Proudhon, Pierre-Joseph. "The Federative Principle." *The Anarchist Library.* https://bit.ly/3BedOQs.

Radnika, Dan. "Rojava: The Fraud of a Non-existent Social Revolution." *Libcom.* June 27, 2017. https://bit.ly/3ToGH3t.

Rancière, Jacques. *Hatred of Democracy.* London: Verso, 2014.

_____. "Jacques Rancière on the Gilets Jaunes Protests." *Verso*. February 12, 2019. https://bit.ly/2X45ht9.

_____. *Nights of Labor: The Workers' Dream in Nineteenth Century France*. Philadelphia: Temple University Press, 1989.

Reclus, Elie. *La Commune de Paris, au jour le jour, 1871, 19 Mars–28 Mai*. Paris: Schleicher frères, 1908.

Rocker, Rudolf. *Nationalism and Culture*. Montreal: Black Rose Books, 1997.

Roussopoulos, Dimitrios, ed. *Participatory Democracy: Prospects for Democratizing Democracy*. Montreal: Black Rose Books, 2003.

_____. *The Rise of Cities*. Montreal: Black Rose Books, 2017.

Roussopoulos, Dimitrios. *Political Ecology: Beyond Environmentalism*. Porsgrunn: New Compass Press, 2015.

_____. "The Democratic Project of Milton Parc." *Trise*. https://bit.ly/3Awd07E.

Ross, Kristin. *A Coffee with Kristin Ross: On the Continuations of May '68*. Athens: Babylonia, 2019.

_____. *Communal Luxury: The Political Imaginary of the Paris Commune*. New York: Verso, 2015.

_____. *May '68 and its Afterlives*. Chicago: University of Chicago Press, 2002.

_____. "Nothing and Everything: The Zad Victory." *Verso*. January 22, 2018. https://bit.ly/3BqDLez.

_____. *The Emergence of Social Space*. London: Verso, 2008.

_____. "The Long 1960s and 'The Wind from The West.'" *Crisis & Critique* 5, no. 2 (November 2018): 325.

Russell, Bertrand. *In Praise of Idleness*. New York: Routledge, 2004.

Sandbrook, Richard. "Why Polanyi and Not Marx?" *Progressive Futures Blog*. May 2, 2015. https://bit.ly/3cMzhXk.

Sadler, Simon. *The Situationist City*. Cambridge: MIT Press, 1999.

Saleh, Yassin al-Haj. "The Syrian Cause and Anti-Imperialism." *Yassin al-Haj Saleh*. May 5, 2017. https://bit.ly/3RashBU.

Sennett, Richard. *The Fall of Public Man*. New York: W. W. Norton & Company, 1992.

Shultz, Lynette. "Educating for Global Citizenship: Conflicting Agendas and Understandings." *The Alberta Journal of Educational Research* 53, no. 3 (2007).

Sinclair, Marshall. "Why the Self-Help Industry is Dominating the US." *Medium*, February 24, 2019. https://bit.ly/3AUXhiI.

Sitrin, Marina. "Recuperating Work and Life." *Roar*. https://bit.ly/3CSIWpZ.

Smucker, Jonathan. "What's Wrong with Activism." *Films of Action*. May 15, 2019. https://bit.ly/3QPA3kY.

Snowball, Timothy. "The United States is Not a Democracy, and It Wasn't Meant to Be One." *The Hill*. October 29, 2018. https://bit.ly/3RB2GlU.

Stavrides, Stavros. *Common Space: The City as Commons*. London: Zed Books, 2016.

Strangler, Cole. "What's Really Behind France's Yellow Vest Protest?" *The Nation*, December 7, 2018. https://bit.ly/3U7DJRg.

Straume, Ingerid S. & Giorgio Baruchello, eds. *Creation, Rationality and Autonomy: Essays on Cornelius Castoriadis*. Aarhus: Aarhus University Press, 2013.

Tarinski, Yavor, ed. *Enlightenment and Ecology: The Legacy of Murray Bookchin in the 21st Century*. Montreal: Black Rose Books, 2021.

Tarinski, Yavor. "Self-Limitation and Democracy," *Public Seminar*. February 7, 2018. https://bit.ly/3Aree4h.

_____. "Sortition and Direct Democracy." *Libcom*. February 4, 2015. https://bit.ly/3LfLIHK.

_____. "Interview with Kristin Ross." *Babylonia*. May 25, 2018. https://bit.ly/3L7YTdY.

Taylor, Charles, et al. *Reconstructing Democracy: How Citizens are Building from the Ground Up*. Cambridge: Harvard University Press, 2020.

Tax, Meredith. "Supporting Dictators is not Anti-Imperialism." *Roar*. June 26, 2019. https://bit.ly/3wwec9V.

Toney, Jason, ed. *Take the City: Voices of Radical Municipalism*. Montreal: Black Rose Books, 2021.

"The Battle for Attica Square–Greece." 2010. https://bit.ly/3QuA9hG.

Tsolakidou, Stella. "The Police in Ancient Greece." *Greek Reporter*. May 30, 2013. https://bit.ly/3AU06SD.

Wakeman, Rosemary. *Practicing Utopia: An Intellectual History of the New Town Movement*. Chicago: University of Chicago Press, 2016.

"What Is Social Ecology?" *Institute for Social Ecology*. https://bit.ly/3q95ivC.

Whitehouse, David. "Origins of the Police." *Libcom*. https://bit.ly/3ctjyw9.

Wright, Erik Olin. *Envisioning Real Utopias*. London: Verso, 2010.

Wright, Erik Olin & Archon Fun, eds. *Deepening Democracy: Institutional Innovations in Empowered Participatory Governance*. London: Verso, 2003.

Virno, Paolo. *Deja Vu and The End of History.* London: Verso Books, 2015.

"'Yellow Vests' Open a New Front in The Battle: Popular Referendums." *France 24.* December 17, 2018. https://bit.ly/2EJOLsq.

Zizek, Slavoj. "Slavoj Zizek on Democracy." November 23, 2016. https://bit.ly/3x58wEt.

Ask your local independent bookstore
for these titles or visit blackrosebooks.com

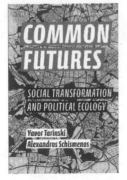

Common Futures:
Social Transformation and Political Ecology
Yavor Tarinski and Alexander Schismenos

Paperback: 978-1-55164-773-9
Hardcover: 978-1-55164-775-3
eBook: 978-1-55164-777-7

Political Ecology:
System Change Not Climate Change
Dimitrios Roussopoulos

Paperback: 978-1-55164-634-3
Hardcover: 978-1-55164-636-7
eBook: 978-1-55164-638-1

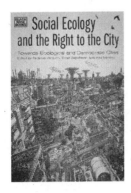

Social Ecology and the Right to the City:
Towards Ecological and Democratic Cities
Federico Venturini, Emet Değirmenci, and
Inés Morales, eds.

Paperback: 978-1-55164-681-7
Hardcover: 978-1-55164-683-1
eBook: 978-1-55164-685-5

Take the City:
Voices of Radical Municipalism
Jason Toney, ed.

Paperback: 978-1-55164-727-2
Hardcover: 978-1-55164-729-6
eBook: 978-1-55164-731-9

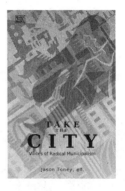